AF723315

# HOW TO BE A LAW PROFESSOR GUIDE

# HOW TO BE A LAW PROFESSOR GUIDE

## FROM GETTING THAT FIRST JOB TO RETIREMENT

**RONALD W. EADES**

PROFESSOR OF LAW AND DISTINGUISHED UNVERSITY SCHOLAR
LOUIS D. BRANDEIS SCHOOL OF LAW
AT THE UNIVERSITY OF LOUISVILLE
LOUISVILLE, KENTUCKY

**VANDEPLAS PUBLISHING**

**UNITED STATES OF AMERICA**

How to be a law professor guide: from getting that first job to retirement
Eades, Ronald W.

Published by:

**Vandeplas Publishing - July 2008**

801 International Parkway, 5th Floor
Lake Mary, FL. 32746
USA

www.vandeplaspublishing.com

ISBN: 978-1-60042-051-1

# CONTENTS

# PREFACE

Law schools graduate tens of thousands of new lawyers every year. Many of them consider returning to law school as a law professor. The law professor job looks like a great career. In fact, it is a great career. For some of us, we believe that everyone wants that job. If everyone does not want that job, they should. Being a law professor is a wonderful way to spend a life. Since so many people seem to hold the position of law professor, it would seem to be an easy job to obtain and keep. It is a little harder to get into the law teaching profession then it would appear.

After teaching in a law school for over 30 years, I decided to try to write down what it is like to get that first law teaching job, stay in the law teaching profession and manage to have a good time doing it. This book is the result of that effort.

It is hoped that this book will help those thinking about looking to be a law professor. I don't think anyone should just jump into that career without giving it some careful thought. If, however, you decide that being a lifelong law teacher is the right career for you, then good luck. If you are successful, you will enjoy it.

Ronald W. Eades
June 1, 2008

# CHAPTER 1 - DOES EVERYONE WANT TO TEACH IN LAW SCHOOL?

## A. Many People Think About Law Teaching

### i. I've Been Asked About it Before

I started teaching in law school in 1977. After just a few years on the job, I discovered some very interesting things. First, almost everyone I talked to outside of the legal profession had either been to law school for a short period of time or thought they might like to go to law school. At first, I offered advice on going to law school. I would suggest getting new information about law schools, starting over, taking the LSAT, applying, or just starting back over in law school at the point the person dropped out. That information is generally available and I was not providing much help. Those that were really interested in attending law school really wanted me to help them get admitted to the school where I taught. When I explained that I just did not have that kind of authority, the conversation usually changed to something else.

I also discovered that many people I met within the legal profession had given some thought to going into law teaching. Almost every lawyer I met had thought about going into law teaching at some time or another in his or her career. Law students or new graduates, practicing lawyers, judges and retirees have approached me about how one gets into law teaching. In those conversations I have discovered that a lot of those prospective "profs" have had a lot of reasons for wanting to get into law teaching. Some of those reasons were good, some were not so good. I have, at times, given personal advice to those who really thought they wanted to find that law teaching job.

After some thought, many conversations and a lot of years, I decided to write down my ideas on the law teaching profession. I was a law teacher at an accredited law school for over 30 years. I got the first job, made it through the tenure decision, taught, wrote, traveled, and even won some awards from the law school and the university. In short, I was able to enjoy the years as a Professor of Law and have some degree of success.

This book is an attempt to cover those ideas. It should explore first why different groups of people would want to be a Law Professor. If the reader is still convinced he or she wants to go that route, the book will attempt to give advice on how to find that first job. Finding the first job is not the end of the journey. It is only the start of it. Getting through the tenure decision and holding on to the job is the first big challenge. Hopefully, this book will provide some guidance on how to accomplish that stage. After that big tenure decision has been mastered, there are still the long years of enjoying the profession ahead. This book will give some ideas about how to spend a life enjoying law teaching. Finally, all good things must come to an end. Partial retirement, full retirement and continuing to work are all options for the law teacher. The end of the book will offer some tips on that.

After many years of thinking about and teaching law, I have probably learned that I better provide some disclaimers. There are around 200 law schools in the United States. They do not all have openings for new law professors every year. Some of the openings that are available are designed for people who have been in law teaching already. There are hundreds of people who actively pursue law teaching jobs every year. Some return year after year to look for such a job. Finding and keeping a law school teaching job is very difficult. Those with the strongest resumes probably get the most attention. Even those with excellent resumes, however, do not always get positions. Matters such as the state of the economy, who is actually hiring, what types of positions are open, what courses do those schools need to have taught, where is the candidate willing to move, and just how good are the interviewing skills of the prospective law teacher are just some of the variables that seem destined to keep many people out of the law school teaching profession. Spending substantial time and money on seeking a law school teaching job is probably not a good investment of either. The odds of getting a good return on the money spent in that search are not good. Anyone who is considering looking into a career in law teaching is strongly advised to keep other options open. For the vast number of people who seek law teaching jobs, the result is that they fail in that endeavor. Very few of the law teaching job seekers find that first position and then manage to remain in law teaching for a whole career.

If having been warned that the odds are stacked against getting a law teaching job, some people still want to pursue such a job, this book may offer some insight. It will try to offer my views based on my own experiences. Law schools and law teachers are all different. Other law teachers have had different experiences, and would offer different advice. After reading this book, the truly serious seeker of a law teaching job may want to gain even further information. Find several current law teachers and get their advice. Find as many different points of view as possible. With the variety of law schools and law teachers that are in the United States, differing information and opinions will be helpful.

Before getting to the real advice, it is important to talk about who should be considering jumping to law teaching. As noted above, everyone associate with law thinks about it at some point. For some of those people, it may be the right time. For others, maybe they should wait.

### ii. New Graduates

There are times when law students believe that they would make great law professors. Some believe they will seek that first law teaching job just as soon as graduation is over. Many of those feel that they would have a better understanding of what students go through since they just went through it themselves. In addition, many feel that a recent graduate would be more up to date on the current state of the law since they just finished law school and probably took a bar review course.

It may seem odd, but some new law graduates do go right into teaching almost immediately. There are law schools that run first year writing programs that are staffed almost totally by recent graduates. There may be a senior faculty member over seeing the whole program while recent graduates provide much of the daily work of teaching and grading papers in direct contact with the students. For some future law teachers, this is seen as a way into the profession of teaching.

There is nothing wrong with such internships or graduate teaching assistant jobs, but the best advice is probably to do something else first. Most law students spend three intensive years learning to be a lawyer. With all of that school work having been completed, the recent graduate should go out and be a lawyer for a while. Get a job with a law firm, a government agency, a public service group or clerking with a judge. Such jobs will introduce the recent graduate to the full range of what it really means to be a lawyer.

One thing that a position as a lawyer may do is convince that recent graduate that being a lawyer is the career path he or she wants to continue following. Many recent graduates have been going to school from the age of 5 or 6 until they graduate from law school. Being a student is all that they know. It is normal for such a person to think that they really want to continue living and working in the academic environment for the rest of his or her life. That person should take a few years out in the other world of legal professions and see what it is like. It may turn out that one of those people who believed he or she wanted to teach will wind up being a judge, gifted agency administrator, or senior law firm partner.

If, after a few years the recent graduate is still convinced that teaching is the life that is desired, there is always time to head back to the academic world. The time out working in the practical legal profession after graduation will not be seen as a detriment during the search for that first law teaching job. Many law schools want their law teachers to have had some law professional experience. Even seeking one of those writing internships will seem easier if the applicant has been in practice for three to five years.

The advice for the law student or recent graduate who wants to be a law professor is simple. It is a little too early. Spend some time out being a practicing lawyer. That time may be spent in any of the numerous law practice fields that are available. If law teaching still looks attractive after working in practice for a few years, that is a better time to start looking for that first teaching job.

iii. Practicing lawyers

Most future law teachers will come from the ranks of practicing lawyers. Many new graduates from law school will get a graduate degree, clerk for a judge, go to a government agency, or work in a law firm and after about 3 to 5 years decide to go into law teaching. Those noted backgrounds seem to work well for future teachers and many law schools like for their new faculty members to have some experience with the actual practice of law. It should also be noted that some actual experience gives the new law teacher a little more credibility with the students.

For all of those reasons, the new graduate from law school ought to assume that some work experience is a real plus when it comes to looking for that first job. That is the primary reason that it was suggested that the new graduate should not try to get that first teaching job immediately after earning that J.D.

Even though some actual law work experience is considered a plus when seeking that first job, staying in the practice of law for a long period of time before seeking that first job begins to erode that advantage. When a lawyer has been in the practice of law for a long period of time and then decides to jump into teaching, several things may have occurred. Those problems will be considered by the prospective law schools. The applicant for a teaching job with an extended practice resume may want to prepare answers for questions that will be asked.

The first problem will be a financial problem for the person looking for the law teaching job. If a person has been in the practice of law for a long period of time, there is a good chance that he or she is earning a substantially large annual income. Law school teaching jobs will not be able to match that income. The person looking to go into teaching will have to be ready to take a substantial income reduction. Even if the person who wants to teach is sufficiently dedicated to be willing to reduce his or her income to enter the teaching profession, law schools will be concerned that salary levels will be an issue. The issue may never be stated by the schools, but may be a reason that offers are not extended. A person with a substantial salary in practice will need to be ready to address the salary issue openly when looking for a teaching job.

There will be some concern by law schools that a practitioner who has been in the practice of law for a long period of time before coming to law teaching is merely looking for a place to retire with a large salary. There is a general feeling among some practitioners that law teacher draw large salaries and do not have to do much work. There are times that practitioners grow weary of the hectic pace of practice and look at law schools as a place to rest. There will be the fear that the practitioner will not prepare for class, but will, instead, just tell stories about old cases. Some practitioners may feel like they learned so much from trying cases there is little preparation to do. A good example might be the teaching of evidence by a seasoned trial attorney. The trial attorney knows there are probably around 40 exceptions to the hearsay rule, but also realizes that only about 10 are used on a regular basis. There may be a fear among law faculty that the practitioner who begins to teach will only talk about those 10 exceptions that have arisen in some old cases. The law faculty members know that the bar exam will require some familiarity with all 40 exceptions. In addition, the well trained student should have been exposed to the broad range of law at least once. There is a concern that the practitioner will do little preparation and tell old stories. Law school faculty members feel like they work hard for low salaries. Any sense that a practitioner is just looking for a relaxed life style will be a major negative in the eyes of the law schools. Practitioners need to be ready to indicate that the reason for moving to teaching is not just to slow down. There needs to be well articulated reasons for the desire to move into that teaching job.

#### iv. Judges

Judges will frequently decide that a law teaching job is a great career move after having been on the bench for some number of years. There is no doubt that most law schools would readily take a retired United States Supreme Court Justice as a member of the faculty. Not all other judges, however, will find law schools as receptive to accepting them as new faculty members.

There is no doubt that most law schools would be glad to accept a judge who stays on the bench and comes to the law school as a part time instructor or part time lecturer. Most law schools would be glad to have such a judge come into the school to offer a few classes on topics of interest to that judge. The schools recognize that judges have a high degree of credibility with students. Also, the presence of the judge adds a level of credibility to the school as a whole. Faculty members even enjoy the presence of judges to have the opportunity to talk about matters of joint interest.

For a judge to come into the school as a regular full time faculty member, however, problems may arise. The financial concerns about salary are probably not as large an issue as with practitioners. Judges do not make as much money as the regular practitioners and could better adjust to the law school salary.

The issue of the appearance of taking a teaching position merely to find a reduced work load, however, will arise with judges. Law school faculty will be afraid that a judge is leaving the bench and wanting to teach as a way to avoid the heavy case load faced by many judges. The fear will be that the judge will not actually do substantial preparation for classes, but will instead merely talk about some old cases that were once before the court. The faculty members will also fear that the judge may not want to engage in the extensive research and writing that is now required of law school faculty. As discussed with the move of practitioners to teaching, law faculty may feel that judges will not fully prepare in order to expose the students to the broad range of issues that arise in different areas. Many of these fears may go unexpressed by the faculty. A judge who decides to move to a law school teaching career should be ready to discuss those issues openly when given a chance.

Finally, a judge that has been on the bench for a long period of time will need to be ready for a different lifestyle in a law school. Judges are used to writing orders and having them carried out. Judges also expect lawyers to argue issues, but then politely accept the judge's ruling. Law faculty members like to argue and disagree about everything. Rarely will a law faculty member follow another's direction. It is considered the best of the academic tradition to continue to debate issues for years. No issue in a law school is ever considered to be settled. There is no rudeness or disrespect that is intended by such behavior; it is just the normal method of expanding the scope of ideas. A judge who decides to enter a law teaching career will have to adjust to never having an opinion fully accepted.

#### v. Retirees

The difficulty with retiring practitioners and judges wanting to enter teaching should already be obvious by the above comments. Some people in the practice of law believe that law faculty members do not work very hard. Law faculty members disagree with that position. If a law faculty member senses that someone wants to move to law teaching as a way to reduce a work load, then there will not be an offer for a full time teaching position. The school may, for particularly well known retirees, offer part time or adjunct positions. If someone is thinking of leaving the practice of law or the bench in order to move to law teaching, that person should seriously think about the reasons he or she wants to make that move. If the reason is to look for an easier way to make money, then there will be little satisfaction in the teaching job. In fact, it may be difficult to find one.

With the concerns that faculty members may have about a retiree entering the teaching profession, any such candidate must be ready to discuss those issues. A retired candidate must be ready to explain his or her expectations about reaching, research and service in the law school. A well articulated explanation of why he or she wants to teach will be necessary.

Since the big question for people wanting to move to law teaching is "why do you want to teach," that should be the next topic to consider. The following material will offer a way to think through that question.

## B. Why Do You Want to Teach?

As I mentioned at the beginning of this chapter, it seems that almost every lawyer I know has asked me at one time or another how to get into law teaching. It looks like a great job. In fact, it is a great job. Before someone decides to dive into the law teaching profession, however, he or she ought to give some serious though as to why that job looks so inviting. It can be a tough, but rewarding career.

### i. It is a Real Job

It is a real job with real law work. It is sometimes thought that university professors do not do very much. Some people outside the university imagined that university faculty members have academic jobs in order to take off from work for long periods of time. A common statement by people to university faculty members is, "It must be nice to have summers off from work." Many law professors teach only two classes a semester. Each class meets three hours each week; so many people assume that law professors only work about 6 hours a week. That work is viewed by many as merely showing up and telling some old stories about cases that were tried many years ago. With all of that misunderstanding, many people assume that law professors only work about six hours a week and only work a few weeks out of the year. That is not what the job entails.

The teaching load for most standard law professor jobs is two courses a semester. That is roughly six class hours a week. That time is scheduled and the faculty member is expected to be there. Law professors teach their own classes and do not have teaching assistants to handle that. Never forget that law students are college graduates already and have usually done well in the prior educational settings. Most of them come to class prepared and expect substantial material to be covered. The faculty member will have to have thoroughly read the material, prepared outside material, and come to class ready to lead the class discussion over complex material. When a faculty member comes to class and tries to just tell a few old stories, the students realize the shortcoming quickly.

Many first year teachers in law school find that new preparations are difficult. It is not unlikely to take approximately five to six hours preparation time for every hour spent in class. Even with that, faculty members frequently find themselves asked questions by students for which that the faculty member did not think about or prepare before class. In addition, experienced faculty members may be called upon to teach a new course. That becomes a new preparation and also requires extensive time commitment to prepare for class.

After a faculty member has taught the same course a few times, it does get a little easier to prepare for class. Preparation for teaching a class the third or fourth time, for example, may only take two to three hours for every hour in class. All of the material must be reviewed and the professor will have to do research to make sure new cases or statutes have not changed the law.

Students like to ask questions outside of class. After the faculty member has spent all of the time preparing for class, then teaching the class, there will be some students who show up at the professor's office to go over the material again. It is expected that university professors will have scheduled and posted office hours. There may be times when those office hours can be used to go through mail, or work on minor projects, but the interruptions caused by students coming to ask questions keeps any major concentrated work from being accomplished.

Law school professors are also expected to do substantial research and writing. The old cliché, "publish or perish," is followed in law schools. New professors may have a little time to get started, but within the first two or three years of teaching, that professor must be producing publications.

Universities expect professors to be engaged in service. That service may be law school committee work, university committee work, or activities with local bar associations. In addition to those activities, there are the general things that everyone is expected to attend. Those include faculty meetings, some alumnae functions, and occasional student functions. All of those activities are necessary to the governance of the school, doing some of the basic administration of the unit, and the smooth running of university life.

If that doesn't seem time consuming enough, then there are exams. A faculty member colleague once said, "Law professors teach for free. The school has to pay us to get us to grade exams." The preparation, administration, and grading of final examinations are the hardest parts of the law professor's job. Grades on examinations are the most critical item to students. A few points on a single exam can make the difference between law review, top 10%

in the class, Dean's list, recruitment by top firms or falling out of that top category. Students quickly learn that the grades they earn in each class are the most important feature of law school. Because of the importance of the grades, faculty members take the examination process very seriously. It takes substantial time to prepare the exams and grade the exams. Although some law schools may have student assistants to help with cite checking for papers, faculty members grade their own exams.

With the class preparation, the exams, research, and service, there is always someone to challenge the quality of the work. Students observe the class performance to learn the material but also to speculate on the quality of the preparation. A student dissatisfied with a final grade, will challenge the quality, fairness and appropriateness of the class, the exam and the grading process. The publication of research invites one's colleagues and the world to challenge positions that have been taken. One of the reasons that research is published is to open it up to free debate. Committee meetings and faculty meetings frequently become debates on the future of the law school. Everyone is ready to challenge the ideas and positions of everyone else. New law professors are subject to review for promotions and tenure. Senior law professors are subject to review for annual raises and distinguished chair opportunities. A law professor cannot take any of the work lightly. Every bit of work that a law professor does is public and open to review and challenge. A new professor cannot come into the job expecting to merely avoid work.

### ii. It Takes a Lot of Hours a Week

As noted above, there is an expectation of quality in the work that a law professor does. Quality work is not produced by working a couple of hours a week. Scheduled classes will take up six hours a week. Preparation for those classes, at least for the new professor, may require an addition 25 to 35 hours a week. Committee assignments, faculty meetings, research and writing add more time to the weekly work load. Keep in mind that some law schools run classes into the night. Some of this work may be done well into the evening. Some lawyers feel like they can get out of the long work week by going into teaching. To do the job correctly, long hours must be spent. It will not be uncommon to spend weekends doing the reading for class preparation.

It is true that law schools and universities have long periods of holidays. Most have a spring break, a long break between semesters in December and January, and then the option of a long summer break. Many law professors find those time are filled with doing the research and writing. It is difficult to complete serious research and writing with committee meetings, classes and student questions. Those times when the students are out of the building are perfect for completion of articles. There is just not as much free time as many outside the university believe that there is.

### iii. You Better Enjoy Research and Writing

It would not seem to be that difficult to do a little research and write a law review article. There are over 200 law reviews available for publications and someone is filling them up with articles. In addition, since law professors need to be teaching students, it would not appear that writing some articles would be that important. Those statements, however, are completely wrong.

Law schools and law faculties take the responsibility of doing research and writing seriously. All law schools expect faculty members to engage in a regular course of research and writing. The specific details of the expectation may differ among the many law schools, but the expectation of some research and writing is there. If a new faculty member does not engage in regular research and writing, that faculty member will not receive tenure. Failure to receive tenure means that the faculty member will be fired. For those that engage in exemplary publication activities, they will get higher raises, awards and greater honors. With presence of the "stick" of being fired and the "carrot" of higher pay, it would seem that doing research and writing would be the most frequent activity of law school faculty members.

The work of doing research and writing, however, is much harder then it appears. Several sections of this book will note that there just never seems to be enough time to do the research and writing. After classes, committee work, faculty meetings and all of the other things that take up time, research gets pushed aside. One of the reasons that research gets pushed aside is that it so hard to do.

Research and writing are activities that must be done alone. It is necessary for the law faculty member to sit alone in the library or on the computer and do the extended research to prepare the article. That faculty member must then sit alone to do the writing. After the writing, there will be time spent doing proof reading and re-writing. There will always be opportunities to discuss the research with other colleagues or at conferences. There may also be the opportunity to co-author works. Even with those types of activities, the vast bulk of the time spent on research and writing is time spent alone. Some people just find it impossible to work that many hours alone. For those who prefer to do group projects or group activities, being sequestered alone for the long hours of research and writing is impossible.

For those that need the presence of others, there will never be time found to do the research and writing. Such people will be looking for committees, talking to others in the hallways, volunteering for positions as a faculty advisor to student groups and otherwise finding ways to avoid being in the library alone. Those faculty members will always appear to be busy, but will never complete research and writing projects.

The difficulty of doing the necessary research and publications raises an opportunity for someone thinking of going into law teaching to carefully consider the real nature of the law teaching job. It is not enough for a person to assume that he or she can just endure the research and maybe churn out an article or two. A person thinking about law teaching should consider that this may be a life long career. No one should place himself or herself in a position of deciding they will just endure a major portion of the job. If that law faculty candidate does not actually enjoy and look forward to the research and writing activities, then that candidate should consider other career opportunities. Being unable to fully enjoy research and writing should be considered a disqualification for the job.

### iv. University Politics are Not for the Faint of Heart

Senior law professors have tenure. They cannot be fired except for some narrowly stated reasons. Clearly with the rights of academic freedom and free speech for those working in state supported universities, law professors find it very easy to state their opinions. University and law school administrators have their own series of issues. The administrators must balance the importance of strong academics against the importance of keeping alumnae happy and supporting the athletic department. For the new faculty member that has just been hired, he or she is just trying to stay out of trouble and keep that job.

Conflicts arise frequently and openly in universities. Universities are built upon the idea of challenging old ideas and bringing forth new knowledge. That carries on into the daily life of the university professor. Law professors are lawyers by training and enjoy arguing. Even the most minor conflict may frequently explode into a great debate within a unit. Faculty members and administrators are frequently in conflict over the direction that issues should go. Faculty members are expected to be part of university and law school governance, but administrators have control over the budget. With that division of authority, conflict is to be expected.

Decisions about promotion and tenure for new professors are shared between faculty and administrators. Some look at tenure as the most solid type of job security in the United States. That is probably true. What many do not realize, however, is that tenure is not granted immediately upon being hired. For most new law professors, tenure is not granted for approximately seven years. For that pre-tenure period, the teaching job is probably the least secure of any job in the United States.

Many new law teachers fear that the promotion and tenure decisions will be random. That is not true. Faculty members have all been through the promotion and tenure process and take it seriously. They do, however, take seriously the teaching and research requirements of the job. Classes will be visited by senior faculty members and fully analyzed. Everything that the new professor produces will be read, reviewed and discussed among the faculty. Tenure is not guaranteed.

Even apart from promotion and tenure decisions, many topics within the law school itself will lead to conflict. Law professors like to argue and will argue over anything. No one's opinion is accepted on face value and will be debated at length. No issue is ever considered settled. Law school faculties find it possible to discuss curriculum, promotion and tenure documents, university governance documents, hiring processes, and a multitude of other items on a recurring basis.

Because of all of those issues, people who find conflict to be unsettling may find that university life is too much chaos. A small law firm may realize the need to work closely together to make sure there is a positive bottom line. Even large law firms have profit as a necessity as it strives to help the client. Universities and law schools do not have that clear standard by which all can agree to be measured. That allows all participants to have different views on the ultimate goals. If being ready to debate every issue or, at least, ready to listen to those debates is not something a person wants to do, then that person should seek a career elsewhere.

v. It is Not Retirement with a Paycheck

For those looking into law teaching as a career because it appears to be an easy way to draw a paycheck and not have to work very hard, that is clearly a misconception. To do the job right and to be successful at it, substantial work will be required. The initial probationary period before tenure will be difficult and emotional. There is no guarantee that job security will ever be reached.

Some of the following chapters in this book will discuss the long road to job security. A faculty member will be expected to reach a level of adequacy in teaching, research and service. All of those activities will be closely monitored and analyzed by senior faculty members and the Dean. Faculty members who do not reach the level of performance expected by the school will be fired.

The job of a law teacher requires long hours of work and that work is done under close scrutiny. The classes, the published works and the service activities are all done in the public eye. Even after tenure is granted, much of the work that is done continues to be scrutinized by the Dean, the university administrators and the public.

Those who believe that they can do very little work and draw a large paycheck are in for an unfortunate surprise. The hours of work will be long and there will never appear to be enough hours to finish the tasks that need to be done. Unless a person actually wants to do the necessary work, the job of law teacher should not be sought.

### C. It Is a Great Job

With all that was said in the above sections, it may be time to begin to wonder why anyone would want to be a law teacher. Clearly there must be something good about the job. Thousands try to get those jobs every year. Thousands who have tenure decide to stay in the jobs until retirement. The truth of the matter is—It is a great job!!!

### i. Get to Think About What You Want To

One of the best features of being any university professor, including a law professor, is that you get to think about what you want to think about. Every practicing attorney knows what drives the law practice. The issues that the practicing lawyer gets to work on are those issues that a specific client needs answered. There may be times when the legal issues that have an impact on the client are boring or irritating. In fact, there may be times when the client is irritating. The practicing attorney may occasional run across some really interesting little legal issue, but if it does not affect the client, it must be ignored. Unless it affects the client, it is not relevant to the practice of law. The practitioner has agreed to represent the client, and future income depends on representing the client, so the practitioner works on the issues that the client needs to have worked on.

A law professor gets to think about whatever is of interest to him or her. The professor may have to teach some classes that were not the first choice. A certain group of classes must be taught and new professors sometimes get what is left. Most professors get to teach a course or seminar that is exactly what they want. Senior professors can keep moving around in the curriculum of courses until all of the courses are the ones they want.

Even though not every course that is taught is the favorite of the professor, the research and writing can be any topic that the professor wants to cover. There is neither a client nor billable hour that is dictating the issue that must be researched. There are also a sufficient number of law reviews being published that almost any topic can get into print.

While any topic is open to research, law professors also frequently find that they can find teaching materials and research ideas from the front page of the morning newspapers. A law professor is not bound to follow the wishes of a client, but can teach, think and write about the current issues of the day. In addition, the law professor can take any position on those current issues. Whether that position is left, right or middle of the road, academic freedom encourages the professor to seek new solutions.

The law professor, however, does not have to think about current issues. The study of legal history is a large, grand and growing field. A new law professor may, for example, decide to devote a career to understanding trover, detinue and the impact those doctrines had on the development of personal property ownership rights.

For those who like to think the great thoughts, research and write, this feature of being a law professor may be sufficient to overcome all of the difficulties with the job. The field of study for the law professor is limited only by that law professor's own imagination.

#### ii. Get to Work With Bright People

It is amazing that most university professors rarely think about this aspect of the job. There are not many jobs in the United States where you get to work with only the most intelligent and well educated people around you.

##### 1. Students

Law students are college graduates. They all had to finish college and they all did well. In addition, they all are motivated to work hard in law school in order to be successful in the future. It is amazing how exciting it can be to teach a class in front of such bright people. Such people frequently see insights and are able to raise questions that are beyond what is expected. The excitement of watching those bright students learn new material and new skills is gratifying.

Law schools in the past 30 years have also been serious about making sure that the class of students in each law school is diverse. Although there is probably more work to be done on that issue for some schools, the ability to work with bright students from diverse backgrounds adds to the quality of the life of a law professor.

### 2. Faculty

Although law faculty members can argue at times, it clearly adds to the job to be able to talk and share ideas with colleagues. There is an old joke that some lawyers find funny. The joke concerns what happens to law students after they graduate, and the sense is that jobs have something to do with grades that were earned. The joke is usually told something like, "The 'A' students make law professors. The 'B' students make judges. The 'C' students make money." There is some measure of truth in some of that joke.

Law professors usually did very well in law school. Others may debate whether such people would have made good practitioners, but that is not the topic of this book. Since most law professors did very well in law school, a professor's colleagues are bright people. If you wanted a group of people with which to debate a complex legal issue, then you could not hope for a better selection of people then a law faculty.

As with students, law schools have been making an effort to create a diverse law school faculty. Having the opportunity to engage in meaningful debate with a diverse, well educated, intelligent group of people is clearly one of the joys of being a law professor.

## iii. Make Your Own Schedule

It was noted earlier about the long hours that can arise with being a law professor. One of the good things about those long hours is that you may set the timing of many of those hours yourself. Classes will have to be set in order to be consistent with the needs of the law school and university. Much of the rest of your work, however, can be accomplished on your schedule.

One of the things that law professors must accomplish is the research, writing and publications. There is very little in the job of research that requires that to be done at any one time. Research can be done on a computer with access to the internet. Articles can be researched and written at night, on weekends or during the summer. There will be self imposed deadlines, but the exact timing of the work is up to the professor.

Those in the practice of law may frequently find that their schedule is changing. Cases get set and then dismissed. Motions get set for argument and then continued. It seems that the schedule changes constantly. For the law professor, the schedule can be set well in advance. The class schedule must be set before students register. It is clearly the norm to have a class schedule a year in advance. Having that clear schedule allows the professor to schedule research and service at convenient times.

There is an indirect benefit to having such great control over the schedule. A law professor can have a life outside of the law school. Practitioners frequently find it difficult to do anything other then take care of the firm. The law professor can get a firm schedule and live a normal life.

That indirect benefit may allow for several things. The professor may find time to travel and research topics not otherwise possible. The professor may opt to teach summer school some years and not others. The professor may opt to visit other law schools for short teaching assignments. The professor may also spend time with the family. The university professor may be able to drop children off at school or pick them up in the afternoon. Getting away from the work for a few hours is usually possible.

### iv. Work in a General University Environment

One of the great benefits to being a law professor is that most law schools are part of a general university environment. Universities have strong libraries, music departments, live theater, and even sports. Law professors find it possible to take advantage of the arts and entertainment on a regular basis.

Universities also offer classes in every topic. Many universities may also offer those classes free or at a reduced rate to faculty members and their families. Many law professors may decide to take a class to learn a language, learn a musical instrument or just learn about wine appreciation.

The university will also have faculties in all of those topics. It is possible to do joint teaching and research with those other faculty members. Law professors may find that some research in a comparison of law and some other topic is really what they want to do. By checking with other units on campus, the law professor can find a faculty member somewhere that is interested in that same comparison.

Although the life of a law professor may not be as easy as some outside the profession believe it to be, for the right person, it is a great life. A law professor has the chance to study and learn news things on a daily basis. The opportunity to discuss great topics with other bright people is a regular part of the job. It is also possible to take advantages of travel, the arts and entertainment offered by the university as a whole. In short, you get to be a student; you get paid for it; you just don't have to take exams anymore.

### D. Try to Provide Some advice

If you are still convinced that you want to be a law professor, then the rest of this book will try to offer you some advice. Like most professions, there are secrets of the trade that a person needs to know before looking for that job. It is not that law professors intend to keep things secret, those little issues have just developed over time. Those in the profession have learned to live with them by experience. Getting a little information about those issues before you start may be helpful.

i. How to Get that First Job

One thing the book will try to do is tell you how law professors get that first job. There are a lot of people who seek law teaching jobs every year. There are only a finite number of law teaching jobs. There are, for example, about 200 accredited law schools in the United States. They do not all have openings ever year. Law teaching jobs are limited. There is no guarantee that you can get one. It is hoped that this book can give you some ideas about how to seek that first job.

ii. How to Stay in Law Teaching

As noted earlier in this chapter, tenure is wonderful job security. The pre-tenure period, however, may be about 7 years and has very little job security. Each law school has its own tenure process rules, but most have very similar expectations. There will be sections of this book that will help you work through that tenure process. Hopefully, you will not only get that first job, you will keep it.

iii. How to Enjoy it Along the Way

The pre-tenure years are somewhat stressful. It is difficult to really enjoy the work if a person is constantly in fear of losing the job. In addition, many law professors do not know what to do after they get tenure. They suddenly find themselves with an expectation of working another 25 to 35 years and really are not certain what to do. The life and work of a law professor is meaningful and can be fun. It is hoped that this book will help provide some insights on how to find the fun aspects of the job. After 31 years of law teaching, I cannot claim to have enjoyed every minute, but I did enjoy most of the days.

### E. Why Did I Think I Could Write This Book

I began my law teaching career in 1977. I talked to a few law teachers before I began to look for that first job and continued to talk to mentors and friends along the way. The friends and mentors provided tremendous help and are probably responsible for any of the success I have had. It would have been helpful, however, to have a good overview of the whole world of law teaching when I first began thinking about seeking such a career. I wish I had found a book early in my career that gave me some suggestions on how to get that first job and then be successful in it. I think it would have been reassuring to see the whole picture as I worked through the different stages of the career. I hope this book will provide that overview.

Most of my advice comes from my own experiences. My own career includes a law degree and a graduate degree in law. I have taught at the same law school for my whole career. That law school is a state supported public institution. During the course of my career, I've had the opportunity to take short visiting assignments at law schools in foreign countries. I have enjoyed the research and writing aspects of law teaching. During the career, I have written and had published numerous law review articles, books and book reviews. I have also had the opportunity to make conference presentations, service on law school, university and civic committees. I have even been able to participate in state wide law reform issues. The activities have been sufficient to win awards for teaching and research. My thought in preparing this book was that I might be able to provide some insight for others who hoped to reach some of those same goals.

There are about 200 accredited law schools in the United States and every one of them has numerous faculty members who could have written this book. One of the difficulties is that every faculty member has had slightly different experiences while going through the career and may offer slightly different advice to people seeking to enter it. My advice is, of course, based upon my experiences. There will probably be other law faculty members who will look at particular parts of this book and say, "I wouldn't do it that way."

Because other faculty members may offer different advice, I have done several things to try to be able to recommend courses of conduct beyond my own experiences. I have talked to other law school teachers over the years at my own law school and from other law schools. I hope I have been able to include those observations in this book. In addition, I have recommended throughout this book that any new law teacher should seek advice from his or her own mentors. Conditions will change by location and time. The specific needs of a law school may dictate slightly different expectations. A new law teacher would do well to work closely with local colleagues in order to reach success. This book should provide a good overview of the law teaching profession, but a new faculty member will want to seek additional specific advice from those who have authority over his or her career.

There is one complaint that will surely come about this book. The advice it in will appear too conservative or safe. Throughout the book, the advice suggests doing things the way they have always been done. It also suggests that a new faculty member should seek out senior colleagues and follow the advice that is given. There is no doubt that there are things about legal education that need to be changed. Intelligent, imaginative law teachers are needed to make changes in law schools. There may be some concern that if all new faculty members merely follow the path that previous faculty members have taken, change will never occur. The complaint, therefore, is that this book does not advocate sufficiently for new faculty members to come in and demand those changes.

I accept that complaint and merely note that the purpose of this book is more limited. The purpose of this book is to help people wanting to get into law teaching reach that goal. It is designed to provide a careful, safe route through the difficult issues of finding a job and reaching tenure. There will be some new faculty members who will come to the teaching profession, demand change and then be fired or remain unhappy throughout a career. For those who follow a path to finding a job and reaching tenure in the safest way possible, the opportunity to make changes is easier after the grant of tenure.

The questions of where should legal education go in the future and what needs to be changed are not within the framework of this book. Those issues should be addressed but would be the topic of another work.

# CHAPTER 2 - FINDING THAT FIRST JOB

## A. What Type of Position is Being Sought?

Many people who view Universities from the outside do not realize that there are numerous different types of positions within that University. It is assumed that all faculty members are exactly the same. Nothing could be further from the truth. Faculty members may be part time or full time. They may be adjunct, visitor, contract or tenure track. Understanding some of those basic differences is necessary in order to determine exactly how someone is to go about getting that first job. Getting a position as a full time, tenure track faculty member is completely different from getting a position as an adjunct. Fully understanding the differences and then seeking the exact position that is desired is necessary for anyone entering law school teaching.

One additional point on this issue has to be taken seriously. Frequently people outside of universities do not consider that the exact title that is used is that important. In a casual conversation, all faculty members may be referred to as "Professors." Faculty members within a university and a law school feel that the exact title is very important.

A lawyer may be practicing law in a city where there is a law school. After some contacts with the Dean of the law school, that lawyer may be offered a position to teach one class a year in some special area. It is not uncommon, for example, to offer such opportunities to trial lawyers to teach a class in trial practice. If the lawyer accepts this position, the lawyer will be paid a small fee to teach that class. Most law school will refer to this position as an "Adjunct Professor." Many such lawyers do not really consider that terminology important. Not understanding the differences, that lawyer may refer to him or herself as a "Professor." In fact, the lawyer may begin to note on his or her resume that he or she is a "Professor" at the law school. It is common for lawyers who teach an occasional class at a law school to say that they are on the faculty at the law school. The full time faculty at the law school will notice this error. As long as the lawyer continues the practice of law and only teaches that one course a year as an "adjunct," then it really does not matter.

Assume, however, that the lawyer decides that teaching that one course a year is so much fun, that he or she wants to become a full time faculty member. That lawyer may notify the law school where he or she has been teaching or even send out resumes to law schools nationwide. That resume may still contain the listing under job experience as "Professor." It may even say something like, "on the faculty at law school." Any existing faculty member will know that the term "Professor" or "on the faculty" implies full time, tenure track position. When a faculty member that reads the resume, inquires about the teaching experience and realizes that it was teaching one class a year as a part time, adjunct, that will look like a false statement on a resume. A false statement or even a perceived false statement on a resume will eliminate any possibility of getting that first position.

If a person is serious about entering the law school teaching profession on a full time basis, then that person must make sure he or she understands the different types of positions. It is also important that if the applicant has any prior teaching experience, that teaching experience must be accurately represented on the resume. If the applicant has any doubt as to the exact title that should be used, he or she should call the Dean where the position was held and ask about the name of the specific title. It may seem like a minor point to one looking for a position. To many faculty members, the different titles are earned and reflect years of work. To casually use the wrong title will be seen as a serious mistake.

### i. Part Time or Full Time

One of the initial decisions that must be made by a person wanting to teach in a law school is whether that person wants a full time or part time job. The first chapter of this book points out the nature of a full time law school teaching position. Such a position assumes that the faculty member is devoting his or her total career activities to the law school. That faculty member will be engaged in teaching, research, publications and service to the institution. It is also assumed that the faculty member will not be continuing to practice law on a regular basis outside of the law school. It may be possible for a full time faculty member to occasionally engage in some paid consulting or to provide pro bono legal services, but those activities will be limited.

A part time position is usually in the nature of an adjunct position. The person will be teaching one or two courses a year at the law school. Those courses may be narrow specialty courses that are offered as seminars or skills courses. A person is usually asked to teach that course because they are known to have extensive experience in that area. Ordinarily, that part time position will not have any other law school responsibilities attached to it. Law school part time positions usually do not have research or service commitments. This, of course, allows the part time faculty member to do whatever else they want with the time they are not teaching the class. Most part time faculty members in a law school are full time practitioners or judges who offer one course a year as a way to provide a service to the law school.

In universities generally, many units may utilize numerous part time faculty on a regular basis. Some faculty members throughout a university may spend their whole teaching careers holding a series of part time positions at different institutions. If they are in a city with several colleges, such faculty members may have part time positions at several different institutions at the same time. Law schools do not work that way. Most of the faculty at a law school is full time. The major accreditation organization, The

American Bar Association, will actually impose limits on the use of part time faculty by law schools.

It is important, therefore, for a person to decide what he or she wants the rest of their life to look like. If that person is committed to becoming a law school faculty member, and that commitment means giving up other forms of outside work, then full time faculty is the appropriate position choice. If, however, the person wants to continue the practice of law while picking up extra money while teaching some classes, then seeking a part time position is the appropriate route.

The importance of that distinction cannot be stressed enough. There have been lawyers who taught a few classes at a law school and thought it looked like easy money. Some would even think, “The full time faculty teach four classes a year and I already teach two classes a year. I should go ahead and get a full time position and really make a lot of money.” They would try to get a full time position, but then never sever their ties with the practice. As the first chapter of this book indicated, the research and service commitment, to say nothing of preparing for new classes in areas in which the person is not a specialist, is very time consuming. There is not enough time to be a full time law faculty member and a practicing attorney. Attempts to do both will lead to great dissatisfaction among the faculty colleagues, the students and the law school administration. It is likely that such a person would not receive tenure.

It is also possible that practicing lawyers or judges will decide to “ease” into the teaching of law. They may believe that they can start as a part time faculty member, show the school they have real talent, and then move into a full time position when one is open. That scenario rarely happens. It may seem unfair, but law schools rarely invite part time faculty members to join the faculty full time. Most law schools will do a national search for a candidate when the school has an opening. Teaching one or two courses a year in the hope of convincing the school to offer a full time position is rarely a realistic proposition. If a faculty member has been teaching a course on a part time basis and decides to enter the full time teaching of law, that person should apply for positions nationally and be ready to relocate.

ii. Adjunct, Visitor, Contract, Clinic, or Tenure Track

There are other terms and position types that should be understood before seeking that first faculty position. Terms such as adjunct, visitor, contract position and tenure track are probably the most important. It is also necessary to discuss some of the distinctions that many law schools make among substantive course teachers, clinical instructors, writing instructors, and librarians.

The position of adjunct professor of law has already been discussed in several places in this work. In a law school setting an adjunct professor is usually a practicing attorney or judge who is asked to teach one or two courses a year in the law school. That teaching assignment will usually be for specialty courses for which that lawyer or judge has extensive experience. Many adjuncts teach such courses as trial practice, or tax court practice. Depending on the expertise within the full time faculty ranks, an adjunct may also be asked to teach Patent law or Anti-trust. Law schools use adjuncts to fill in classes that need someone with extensive expertise and, due to relatively low student enrollments, usually will not justify hiring a full time person to teach in that area. Adjunct faculty members are part time faculty and are usually paid a very low fee to teach the class. Many law schools look upon adjuncts as committed alumnae who are teaching the class as a favor to the law school. For a full time practitioner or judge who wants to teach one or two classes a year, but have no other work commitments to the law school, the position of adjunct is the appropriate choice.

The term "Visiting" professor is commonly heard in universities and law schools. A visiting professor is usually a person who holds a full time, tenure track position at a law school and has been invited to another law school to teach full time for one semester or one year. This may occur for several reasons. A law school may have a few faculty members away from the school on leave or sabbatical and need someone to fill a few courses for one year. Some law schools use visiting professors for what is called a "look see." That law school may know it will have a vacancy in a particular area in a couple of years. Rather than merely advertising and searching nationally for someone to take the spot, the law school may invite a visitor or two to come to the law school for a semester at a time. After getting to see that visitor perform for a semester or full year that law school can then decide whether it wants to offer that person a position. It should be obvious that a visiting position is not one that a first time job applicant for a law school teaching job will seek. They are filled by people already in the law teaching profession. Since visitors are used to fill gaps in schedules, school look for faculty members among the experience professors of other schools.

For most people looking for a position in law teaching, the important distinction is between being on tenure track and being a contract professor. While looking for a position, it can be assumed that most of the positions will be tenure track. Some law schools are limiting commitments for some positions by making them contract based. During the interviewing process, it is a good idea to ask about the tenure process. This will be an easy way to determine whether the position is actually a tenure track position. It is important, however, to make sure which is being offered.

A tenure track position is what most people associate with university faculty. It is the process followed in most law schools. A new faculty member will be hired as a probationary employee. That faculty member will be on a tenure track, but not yet tenured. During that probationary period, which may range from 4 to 7 years depending on the law school, the faculty member will be reviewed by a personnel committee. That committee will be charged to determine whether the new faculty member is meeting the teaching, research, and service requirements. After the prescribed period, the faculty member will be considered for tenure and, hopefully, granted tenure. Once tenure is received, it is a lifetime appointment. The faculty member cannot have the position terminated in the absence of some serious wrongdoing.

Although usually a tenured faculty member cannot be fired except for some serious wrongdoing, any faculty member may be fired due to emergency economic reasons. The economy of the United States goes through regular cycles. During down economic cycles, universities and law schools tend to suffer the same downward economic trend. During extreme periods of economic problems, law schools may find it necessary to discharge untenured or even tenured faculty members. Tenure is viewed as a life time appointment, but it is not a guarantee against recessions.

Tenure track positions are usually used for faculty who teach the substantive law classes. By substantive law courses, law schools think in terms of such courses as torts, contracts, civil procedure, evidence, tax, and all of those other courses that students must take in order to graduate and take the bar examination. Tenure track positions, therefore, have the greatest job security. In addition, full time, tenure track positions usually have the highest salaries.

Contract positions do not result in tenure. When a faculty member is hired in a contract position, the period of employment is usually 1 to 3 years as clearly stated in the contract. During the period of the contract, the faculty member would have a contract right to the position. The position could not be terminated without following the language of the contract. At the conclusion of the contract, period, however, the faculty member does not have to be rehired. When a law school uses a contract method of employing faculty members, it may reserve the right to extend the contract, but there is no requirement for that to be done. When a law school decides to hire faculty members on a contract basis, it is usually done for faculty members who will be teaching in the clinics or in a writing program. Law schools rarely use such an arrangement for faculty members teaching the substantive law classes. With the differences in long term job security between tenure track and contract basis, however, it is important to make sure what type of position is being offered.

It should be obvious that most of the faculty members who teach the substantive law classes in a law school are full time, tenure track or already tenured faculty members. There are, of course, several other types of programs within the law school that students may be required to take or have the option to take. The staffing of those positions may frequently not be full time, tenure track positions.

Most law schools have some type of writing program for the law students. This program usually has its primary focus for first year law students. The students will learn how to use the library and how to do legal writing. Many of the programs will require students to write memos and briefs. Some of those programs even have an oral argument as part of the process. Law schools use a variety of methods to staff the writing program. Some may have a single full time faculty member, either tenure track or contract, that is responsible for the whole program. The daily teaching and grading is then done by recent graduates who have been hired on short term contracts. Some law schools use full time faculty to teach the entire writing program but use contract employment for those positions. A few law schools use a combination of tenure track, contract, and student assistants to teach in the program. Frequently law schools will not expect the writing faculty to have the same level of production of research and service as tenure track faculty.

The absence of a full commitment to tenure track positions in writing programs continues to be a controversial issue for law schools. The details of the controversy are beyond the scope of this book. It is only important for the person seeking a position to understand what the nature of the position will be.

There are times when a person seeking to enter law teaching will believe that taking a writing position may be a way to get started. That person may hope that, after a few years, the law school will then move them over to a tenure track position teaching a broad range of subjects. That rarely happens. Once someone is hired in a law school as a writing teacher it is usually assumed by the law school that the person will remain a writing teacher. There are many dedicated people teaching writing in law schools today. In some ways, that may be the most difficult course in the curriculum to handle. Many of those writing teachers thoroughly enjoy their positions and would not think of teaching anything else. If teaching a writing program is what the new faculty member desires, then seek out the writing positions. The advice is to realize the difference between the writing positions and other types of positions in the law school.

Most law schools have developed clinical programs for students. The clinic may be in a law school facility and offer legal services to actual clients. The law students will assist with providing that legal service under the guidance of a licensed attorney. In order to run these clinics, many law schools hire a clinical professor to act as the clinic supervisor. The clinic supervisor will be a licensed attorney who is able to practice law in that jurisdiction. Since the clinic is in the law school, that clinic supervisor is a faculty member. Most law schools are placing the clinical faculty on a contract basis. In addition, their work requirements may not allow for full summers off and the same holidays as other faculty members. Clinical faculty members are running a law office and must be ready to represent clients. Frequently clinical faculty members do not have the same level of expectations for research and service as tenure track faculty. As with writing faculty, there continues to be a controversy as to whether clinical faculty members ought to be eligible for tenure in a law school. That topic is outside the scope of this book. It is important for someone seeking a law teaching job, however, to be aware of the nature of the appointment.

There are some practicing lawyers that hope to obtain a clinical position and then use it to move into a full time, tenure track substantive law teaching position. That rarely happens. Once a person is hired as a clinical faculty member, the law school will usually assume that person will stay there.

As with writing faculty members, there are many dedicated clinical faculty members who could not imagine doing anything else with their lives. They enjoy working with students while providing a real service to the community. For those that desire that type of position, seek them out. While seeking that position, however, realize the nature of the relationship with the law school and other faculty members.

All law schools have law libraries. The library will have a full complement of employees that manage the library. The Director of the law library usually will have a full time, tenure track position on the law school faculty. Other members of the library staff, however, may not have such a position. The Director of the law library is usually hired in the same way that all other law school teaching faculty members are hired. Other library staff members are hired in a variety of ways. If someone is interested in a position in a law library, he or she should contact a member of a law library and seek information about those opportunities. As with writing faculty and clinical faculty, a member of a law library staff should not assume that he or she can easily use that position to move over into a full time, tenure track position to teach substantive courses. That rarely happens.

There are a variety of other positions in a law school that may seem like a way into law school teaching. Many law schools hire lawyers to act as continuing education directors, student services directors or other such positions. Those positions are usually considered staff and not faculty positions. It is usually not possible to move from one of those positions to a full time, tenure track teaching position.

Although that discussion provides most of the information for understanding the different types of positions within a law school, there are just a few more terms to be understood. For the entering new faculty member, they may not seem important. Within the institution, however, these additional titles are critical.

The typical titles used by law school faculty members are "Assistant Professor," "Associate Professor," and "Professor." Many law schools require the new faculty member to begin as an Assistant Professor. The first promotion will take the person up to the rank of Associate Professor. The second promotion will take the person up to the rank of Professor. Not all law schools require that everyone go through all ranks. Some may start the new faculty member as an Associate Professor. In casual conversation, everyone may be referred to as a Professor. It is wise, however, in resumes, letters, notes or anything else in writing to be sure and use the correct title.

If the internal structure of a law school appears confusing, that is correct. The variety of types of positions and titles is broad. It is important for a new person looking for that first job to know exactly what he or she wants. Once the interviewing process is underway, it is permissible to ask what the normal "tenure process" is in that institution. Every law school will have a document that outlines the number of years and the work expected to meet the terms of promotions to Professor and tenure. Faculty members at a law school realize how important the issues of type of position and probationary process are. The faculty will actually expect that to be a question and will answer it. Since movement within a law school among the different types of position is so rare, it is important to make sure that a new faculty member gets the type of position that is desired.

### B. Basic Credentials

The basic credential for most law school teaching jobs is to have the J.D. degree. A few law schools have created positions in philosophy or some other law related topic which may not require the J.D. but those are rare. For purposes of a general discussion, it should be assumed that a J.D. degree is required. With the number of people looking for law teaching jobs and the relatively few number of openings each year, just relying on the fact of having a J.D. is not enough to secure a position. Law schools will be looking for a much stronger resume.

When a law school judges a resume, it is rare that one particular item will decide all issues. Most law schools are looking for the best candidate that will be able to fill the slot that is open. The following items are areas of accomplishment that law schools will be reviewing for every candidate. Obviously, if a particular candidate is outstanding in every area that is the candidate that will get the offer. For most candidates, the resume is something of a balance. It will be strong in some areas and a little weak in others. If it is weak in all areas, then it is unlikely that candidate will get a position. In addition, obtaining a law teaching position depends on numerous factors other then the basic credentials. Even for the candidate with the perfect background, there is no guarantee of obtaining a law teaching position. If, for example, the national economy is weak and there are very few law school teaching positions available in a particular year, the strength of the resume is irrelevant. Law schools do not create jobs where the do not exist. A person looking for a law teaching job may have an outstanding resume, but find that his or her own interviewing skills seem to limit job opportunities. There are just too many factors that determine who will get the limited number of law teaching jobs that are available to be able to provide any guarantees. The most that a candidate can do is to put together the strongest package that is possible and then try to convince law schools that the resulting resume is one that promises success in law teaching.

i. The Undergraduate Degree

People do not get into law school initially without an undergraduate degree. That means that all candidates searching for a law teaching job will have some type of undergraduate degree. The undergraduate degree is not one of the items of major importantance on the resume when searching for a law teaching job. As with many items on a resume, however, the better that undergraduate degree looks, the stronger the overall resume appears. If a candidate has a strong undergraduate degree, ranked high in the class from a top noted college or university, that should be emphasized on the resume.

There are times when the nature of the undergraduate degree may be important. If the candidate is hoping to offer courses in Jurisprudence or Legal history, a strong undergraduate degree in philosophy or history may help attract attention. If a candidate is hoping to offer courses in patent law, a degree in engineering may be helpful. A person looking for a position should spend some time thinking about whether there is something about the undergraduate degree that can be highlighted.

ii. The Law Degree

The law degree and the performance of the candidate in law school will be one of the major issues to address in the resume. Most law school faculty members feel that graduating with a high rank from a top law school is important in performing well in law teaching. In reviewing candidates for positions it is common for law schools to note the law school that the candidate attended to determine whether that law school was accredited by not only the ABA but also the AALS. It will also be noted as to whether that law school has a chapter of Order of the Coif. Although law schools do not like to talk about the types of national rankings of colleges, universities and law schools that seem to show up in magazines, the national stature of the law school attended by the candidate may also be considered. Of course, the actual performance of the candidate in terms of grades and class rank is important. That attitude may seem unfair to some, but it is one that must be confronted by those seeking law teaching positions.

There are times when a lawyer feels that he or she would be an excellent law teacher because they understand the struggles of the students who do not do well in law school. That type of candidate may have had difficulty with the academic setting, did not graduate high in the class, and now wants to assist that type of student. Most law schools will not consider that type of candidate for the standard tenure track position teaching substantive courses.

There may be times when some difficulties with the law school grades may be overcome. A candidate for a clinical position may be judged by slightly different criteria. The law school will be interested in someone who is able to supervise a practical setting and the exact class rank may not be important.

People looking to teach part time as an adjunct professor will also be judged by different criteria. The law school will be looking for someone to fill in a particular course and experience in that specific area will be critical. The overall class rank will be of less importance.

Generally, a candidate for a law teaching job that had low grades and low class rank is going to find it difficult to obtain a position. Law faculty members like to see new additions to the faculty that did well in law school and did that at a top law school. That fact must be considered by the candidate prior to seeking such a job. If such a candidate wants to continue to pursue a law teaching position, it would be important to strengthen the resume in other areas.

In addition to having high grades in law school, having accomplished the additional extra-curricular activities is also an important feature of looking for a law school teaching position.

Many current law teachers were on the law review of their own law schools. They feel that was an important activity and will expect that new law teachers will have had that experience. If the candidate for a teaching job was on the law review and, in fact, held an editorial position that is considered strongly.

Activities such as participation in moot court and mock trial competitions are also considered important. Law schools realize that students will want those activities to be offered and having faculty members who have participated themselves in those activities is appreciated.

Since law schools will be seeking candidates will strong academic records, membership in honor societies such as Order of the Coif is another important item on a resume. If the law school that the candidate attended had other academic honors or awards, those too should be clearly noted.

As more law schools have added pro bono requirements to their programs, an interest in pro bono activities while in law school should be noted. If a candidate engaged in such activities, completed substantial hours, or provided considerable volunteer time to an organization, it should be noted on the resume.

Law school social activities are usually not considered important to law schools in hiring new faculty. If a candidate was the class social chair or party planner, that probably does not need to be on the resume.

To make a strong resume, a candidate for a position needs to be able to point to strong academic performance while in law school. The resume should be carefully drafted to point out those features that illustrate that strength.

### iii. Judicial Clerkships

Judicial clerkships are a positive feature of a resume when a candidate is looking for a law teaching job. The types of work and connections that a judicial clerk makes are the types of things that law schools feel are important. In addition, law schools like to be able to place their own graduates in judicial clerkships. It is always felt advantageous to have a few prior judicial clerks on the faculty to help place the law school's students.

Law schools would tend to recognize a hierarchy of judicial clerkships. This may also seem unfair to some, but some clerkships are viewed as better indicators then others. Having clerked for a Justice of the United States Supreme Court is, of course, the pinnacle. Such candidates for law teaching jobs usually have no trouble finding one. Below that, clerking for a Federal Circuit Court Judge is well respected. Clerkships with for Federal District Judges are also appreciated but with a little less interest then the others already named.

Many law schools would generally rank a clerkship with a federal judge as better than having clerked for a state judge. If the candidate did clerk for a state judge, the ranking from State Supreme Court down to State Trial judge would also be followed.

Although law schools may find clerking for a federal judge more important then clerking for a state judge, any type of judicial clerkship is considered positive. Whether it is federal or state, a candidate that has such a background should make sure that it is noted on the resume.

### iv. Working as a Lawyer

Some prior practical experience as a working lawyer is also considered a positive feature for a candidate seeking a law teaching job. Law schools feel it is important that, at least, some of the faculty be able to relate theory to real life examples. For faculty seeking clinical positions, the prior work experience will probably be a necessity. For many other law faculty positions, such prior legal experience will be helpful to securing that first law teaching position.

In highlighting the prior law work experience, a few matters should be noted. Law schools like to see prior experience at well known places. A candidate who has worked for a few years at the Department of Justice, the Securities and Exchange Commission, or a major firm in New York or Los Angeles will be sought out. Those are just a few examples, but should provide some idea of how law schools consider this item. Work experience at major federal or state agencies, major public interest organizations, or major law firms should be highlighted on the resume.

v. Prior Teaching Experience

Although it may come as something of a surprise, prior teaching experience is not considered a necessity by law schools looking for new law teachers. Law schools believe that law school teaching techniques are, in some ways, different from other teaching areas. This is probably not totally true since the psychology of learning is consistent throughout the educational fields, but it is a belief held by many in law schools. For that reason, an extensive background in teaching outside of the law area will not be considered important.

Some experience in law teaching may have some slight importance. If a new candidate has been teaching as an adjunct a prospective law school may want to ask some questions about that experience. In fact, there is a good possibility that references will be closely checked to make sure that the experience was a positive one. The absence of such prior teaching, however, will not be considered fatal to the resume.

One positive feature that some prior law teaching experience can provide is an easy way for the candidate to explain why he or she is ready to go to full time teaching. If that candidate felt that the prior teaching experience was positive, then a decision to leave other careers to enter full time teaching seems rational.

### vi. Graduate Degrees

The graduate degree in law raises some interesting questions for the prospective law teacher. Many law schools offer such graduate law degrees and many lawyers decide to get one. There are numerous types of degrees that serve a variety of purposes. Whether such a degree will actually enhance a candidate's chances of obtaining a law teaching job is not an easy question to answer.

#### 1. Types of degrees available

As noted above, there are many types of degrees offered by numerous schools for a variety of purposes. There are degrees in specific subject matters that seem more designed to strengthen the knowledge base of a practicing attorney. An L.L.M. in Tax, for example, may improve the ability of a tax lawyer to work in a complex matter. Graduate degrees in international trade may assist lawyers who find themselves doing contract and corporate work in a global market. Candidates for law teaching jobs may discover that such graduate degrees are helpful to the preparation and presentation of materials in classes in such topics. The graduate degree will provide additional insights and additional credibility to those being taught.

Some graduate programs offer general degrees where the student puts together a range of courses of his or her own choosing. A student could, for example, arrange a program to study Constitutional Law, Legal History, or Jurisprudence. Such topics would be interesting and allow the law school teaching candidate to broaden the knowledge base that he or she has.

The real question that most candidates for law teaching jobs will probably ask, however, is simple. Is the pursuit and attainment of the graduate degree worth the time and expense?

2. Are they worth the time and expense?

Many law schools will look at the attainment of a graduate degree as a positive feature on a resume. Some may even consider the attainment of either a graduate degree or some substantial work experience as a necessity. Such a requirement could be read as wanting the new law teacher to have some type of substantial law experience beyond the basic law school degree. Few, if any, law schools would require the attainment of a graduate degree as a condition of getting or keeping the law teaching job.

Even though such graduate degrees may not be necessary, there are a few helpful features of such degrees. In considering a career move to law teaching, a candidate will want to think about whether obtaining such a degree is helpful.

Getting a graduate degree in law may, for some, strengthen the resume. Law schools like to have law faculty members from top law schools. If a candidate did not graduate from such a top law school initially, but did obtain a graduate degree from such a well known institution, it strengthens the resume.

During the early years as a law teacher, preparing for class, completing committee assignments and still finding time to do research and writing is difficult. The new law teacher that comes right out of a graduate degree program comes with some advantages. Most graduate degrees require a master's thesis. Upon completion of this substantial work, the new candidate for a law teaching job can promptly turn that thesis into one or two law review articles. This will allow that person to get a good start on publications. Frequently the class work in graduate programs will also suggest some topics for research projects. Those topics can also be turned into law review articles in a short period of time. In short, a graduate program can be used to get a good start of the research that a new faculty member is expected to do.

Some graduate programs are designed for people who want to teach in law school. The course work and the master's thesis will provide a good background for the early years of the new law teacher. In addition, such law schools like to see their graduate students placed in good teaching jobs after getting that graduate degree. To that end, some graduate programs make a special effort to assist the graduate students in finding law teaching positions. Having the support of a well respected law graduate program is helpful during the job search phase.

In short, there is no easy answer to whether a candidate for teaching job should get a graduate degree. There is a cost in terms of time and money in obtaining that degree and no guaranteed jobs after the degree is obtained. Someone looking for a law teaching job will have to carefully consider when, in his or her own circumstance, the graduate degree would be a wise investment.

#### vii. Publications

Law schools expect full time faculty members to be engaged in serious research and publications. The failure to do so will result in a faculty member losing the job he or she fought so hard to get. Most law school hiring committees, however, realize that prior to getting that first faculty position lawyers may not have had the opportunity to engage in substantial research that led to publication. The absence of publications from a resume is not an automatic exclusion from the law school faculty job. Law school hiring committees will want to see and hear of some promise of a future commitment to writing, but will not require past publications.

Although a law school will not require publications prior to offering that first job, a record of publications is very useful. Many members of a law school faculty will feel that the best evidence of a future commitment to publications is a past record of such publications. Faculty hiring committees hear numerous candidates each year promise to devote their lives to serious research and writing. Faculty personnel committees are then disappointed each year to watch young faculty members fail to live up to those promises. When a law school is interviewing candidates for a new position, the candidate will, of course, promise to engage in research and writing. If the resume of that candidate reflects that the person has already amassed several publications, it helps the hiring committee be convinced that the promises of future research will be kept. Publications prior to getting that first job are not, therefore, necessary, but they do help convince the law school that the candidate is likely to continue that research work.

Since a record of publications is a nice addition to a resume, so consideration should be given to the type of publications that are most helpful. The best examples that can be included on a resume are substantial law review articles published in recognized law journals. They may include articles that a candidate wrote while a law student and had published in the student's law review. Those are the types of articles that a new law professor will have to write and get published in order to ultimately get tenure. If the candidate for the job has already begun producing such work, then the notice of such publications on a resume is helpful.

There are, of course, other types of publications that should be noted. Practicing lawyers may have the opportunity to publish short articles in local or state bar magazines. Those articles may include discussions of practical issues, new rules, or even book reviews. Such publications should be listed on the resume but will not add substantially to the candidate's value. Many law school faculty members look upon such work as not of the same level of complexity as serious law review articles. Some candidates for jobs may have written opinion pieces or letters to the editor for the local newspaper. Such items will not be considered the same type of effort as a law review article.

Some lawyers will have had the opportunity to write books that are sold to the practicing bar. Obviously the publication of books is recognized by some as a substantial effort that reflects well on the commitment to research and publications. It should be kept in mind that not all law faculty members look upon such books as an appropriate effort for law teachers. Some law faculty members refer to such books as "practice manuals" and feel a faculty member's efforts would be better spent working on law review articles. The presence of such books on a resume, however, should be looked upon by the candidate as a plus. A substantial number of members of the law teaching profession will feel that the books are of value or, at least, reflect a long term commitment to research.

### viii. Make that Resume Accurate

Most of the above information discussed the background that will be viewed by hiring committees when a candidate is seeking that first law teaching job. In seeking that job, the candidate will have to prepare a resume which is frequently referred to as a curriculum vitae in Universities. That resume will form the basis of the initial review of consideration of the candidate. With many more people looking for a teaching position then the number of available teaching positions, that resume is critical. There are a many sources available to help a candidate prepare a good resume. A few special issues, however, should be noted when looking for a law teaching job.

Of primary importance is to make sure that the resume is accurate. Most people recognize that a resume has to be honest and accurate in seeking any type of employment. There are, unfortunately, numerous stories of people making small, untrue statements on resumes. In law teaching, any inaccuracies on a resume, regardless of how small, is considered a major breach. The discovery of an inaccuracy on a resume will result in the candidate not being hired initially and fired if the job was offered. With numerous people looking for the few jobs that are available, hiring committees do not have to work with a candidate with an inaccurate resume. The resume must be absolutely accurate.

There are, in fact, two issues that may be especially troubling when considering the possibility of error in a resume. First, if there is even a hint of error, the hiring committee may decide to stop considering the candidate. Again, with numerous people looking for a very few jobs, hiring committees may decide to discontinue consideration of a candidate with the first hint of error. Such a committee may feel that there is no reason to waste time on such a candidate when there are so many other candidates available. Second, the candidate may not even know why he or she was suddenly dropped from consideration. A member of the hiring committee may have noticed something odd on the resume or called a reference and gotten an inconsistency. The hiring committee may merely drop consideration of the candidate without any explanation. In short, the resume must be absolutely accurate, and it must not even hint of inaccuracy. The presence of any problems will result in consideration of the candidate being discontinued without any opportunity for further explanation.

One of the major issues of concern for accuracy is the completion of degrees. Universities and law schools are in the "business" of granting degrees. As such, those institutions are greatly concerned about the accuracy of claims of degrees held by candidates for positions. In filling out a resume, some people may feel comfortable mentioning a university attended when no degree was received. In an effort to provide complete information, it is probably necessary to note all institutions of higher education that were attended. It is necessary, however, to be clear as to what that relationship was. If an institution was attended for only one year, then the resume must state that clearly. If a degree was obtained from an institution, then the resume should give the years attended, the year graduated and the specific degree earned. It cannot be overstated as to how important clarity on this topic must be.

Law schools will want future faculty members to be committed to research and publications. As such, the presence of publications on the resume will be important. In drafting the resume, accuracy on that issue is also important. The resume should state the name of the article, the name of the publication, a citation to a location where the publication may be found and the date of publication. It is also necessary to be accurate about authorship. If the candidate was the sole author of the article, then the resume may state that fact. If, however, there were any co-authors on the publication, that information is necessary. The failure to report co-authors is considered a serious flaw in the resume.

Candidates for a law teaching job will find it necessary to report past work experience. Again, it is important for this portion of the resume to be accurate. The resume should state the nature of the position and how long it was held. In describing the work that was done in the prior position, do not exaggerate the duties. Be clear as to the exact nature of the job.

In preparing the resume, make sure there are no unexplained gaps in time. Faculty members who are reviewing resumes will notice quickly when there is a two or three year gap in the resume. It is quite possible, for example, that a candidate worked in law for a few years and then did some type of public service work for two years. The resume needs to reflect all of that time. An unexplained gap in the resume will make the reader of the resume wonder what was happening. With many resumes to review, it is easier to discontinue consideration of such a resume rather than try to find out about the gap.

It should be clear that accuracy on the resume is of primary importance. Law schools are educating the future lawyers of America and take the commitment to ethical conduct seriously. Law schools will not risk having a faculty member who carelessly provides inaccuracy on a resume. A candidate for a law teaching position should be sufficiently concerned about even the appearance of honesty that no hint of inaccuracy will appear on the resume. For the candidate that believes a few small exaggerations will not be discovered, that point of view is probably wrong. The law teaching profession is a small community. Most law teachers attend an annual conference each year. Most law teachers have met and know many other law teachers around the country. During the hiring process, references, prior job descriptions, publications, and prior degrees are checked before a position is offered. If there is an inaccuracy on the resume, it will be caught.

## C. Applying for the Position

Now that some information concerning the types of positions has been stated and the basic requirements for the positions have been discussed, it is time to look at how a prospective faculty member would actually apply for a position. This issue may be broken down into two sections. There is a difference in the way that a person would seek a law teaching position with a law school within the local community where he or she currently resides and the way that same person would seek a position in law schools on a national basis. The following sections will discuss looking for that local position and then entering a national search.

### i. Local Positions

Over the years, I have experienced a common occurrence. Lawyers in the city where I lived would call and ask how they could get on the faculty at the law school. For some, the question was that they wanted to teach one course on a part time basis. The answer to that question was easy. Most law schools do hire lawyers to teach one or two courses on a part time basis. As discussed earlier in this chapter, that job position is usually referred to as "adjunct faculty." Those part time positions are usually filled on an "as needed" basis and do not require a lengthy search and interview process. Usually someone within the law school administration will be responsible for hiring "adjuncts" and that is the person to contact.

If the job being sought is as an adjunct, the candidate should call someone at the law school. It would be best to call a faculty member or dean with whom that candidate has had some prior contact. The candidate can explain that he or she is interested in teaching one course, identify the course that is desired and ask who should be contacted. Most faculty members in the law school will know who is responsible for hiring adjuncts. Once the appropriate person is identified, the candidate should contact that person by phone first and then send a letter with resume attached. The resume should highlight why that candidate is appropriate for teaching the specific course.

The appropriate time to apply for a position as a part time teacher, or adjunct, is difficult to specify. Adjuncts may, in fact, be contacted at any time. Frequently, law schools will try to make up the class schedule one or two years in advance. That will require the schedule maker to contact possible adjuncts at an early date and begin to set up a tentative schedule. That may mean that a lawyer will be asked to teach a course but informed that the course is one year in the future. In addition, adjuncts may be hired to fill in a course during an emergency. That may require the schedule maker to look through a file of resumes, call someone at the last minute and ask that person if he or she can start teaching a course in a few days.

Because of the inability to specify a particular time, a candidate for a part time position may feel comfortable to contact the law school about such a position at any time. Contact the appropriate person in the law school by phone and letter. If no position is offered immediately, contact the appropriate person about every six or eight months later. It may even show a little extra interest if the candidate is able to talk with the appropriate person at events that the law school is having in the community. An adjunct position may be offered immediately, within a short period of time or never. The need for adjuncts depends on the nature of interests of full time faculty, whether the courses are being fully covered by such faculty and the courses for which students are actually signing up.

Occasionally a local practitioner or judge will contact a local law school and ask to apply for a full time, tenure track position. That local candidate may decide that he or she would like to enter the teaching profession full time and wants that employment to be in the city where he or she currently lives. It may even be that the local lawyer was a graduate of that law school and wants to go back there to teach. The placement of a local lawyer on the local law school faculty is exceeding rare. Most law schools do not hire local lawyers or the law school's own graduates to teach in the law school.

Law schools, as do most universities generally, have a commitment to a broad definition to diversity. This includes bringing in teachers and scholars from a wide range of other institutions. It is thought by most law schools that the teaching and research missions of the law school is improved by having faculty who graduated from a variety of law schools around the nation and the world. Law schools fear that bringing in local lawyers or local graduates as full time faculty members will result in a narrowing of the educational opportunities for the students.

Even for the candidate looking for a position, moving outside of the local community and away from his or her own law school is in that person's own best interest. When a person moves to another location and another law school, they immediately become a colleague to the faculty that is in place at that law school. The new faculty members may be viewed as a "junior" colleague that will need help and assistance, but they will be viewed as a colleague. If that same candidate takes a position at a local law school or one from which they graduated, there will be faculty members still at the law school who remember that person as a student. That new faculty member will remain something of a "student" in the eyes of that faculty.

If a person is serious about becoming a full time, tenure track law teacher, then the decision should be made to enter the national search. That candidate may make a special effort at a few schools, including one in his or her own hometown, but the search should be national. That national search will accomplish several important goals. It will open up more opportunities for actually finding a position. A positive result may reveal several new job opportunities that were otherwise unseen. It may even demonstrate to the local law school that the candidate has a real commitment to law teaching that would not have been otherwise noticed. Unfortunately, there may be a downside. A national search for a position is more expensive and time consuming. In addition, it may reveal the candidates true ability to obtain a law teaching job. If, after engaging in a national search, no offers are made, the candidate may be able to move to other career opportunities.

ii. National Searches

If the candidate is serious about seeking a full time, tenure track law teaching position, then entering the national search is necessary. Participation in a national search is expensive and time consuming. There is, however, a nationally organized search process that is available to law schools and the candidates who wish to be considered for positions. This national process is organized by the Association of American Law Schools.

The Association of American Law Schools is the primary national organization for law schools and their faculties. In fact, any candidate for a law teaching position should visit the association web site and thoroughly read all information that is offered. A study of this web site will reveal substantial information about law schools in general.

The web site for the Association of American Law schools is:

http://www.aals.org

The address and telephone number for the Association of American Law Schools are:

The Association of American Law Schools
1201 Connecticut Avenue, N.W.
Suite 800
Washington, D.C. 20036-2717
Telephone (202) 296-8851

Each year the Association of American Law Schools offers a national Faculty Recruitment Conference. This conference is usually held in the fall of the year and provides an opportunity for law school hiring committees to meet and hold brief interviews with candidates for law school teaching positions. Anyone seriously interested in seeking a full time law teaching or full time clinical position should consider participating in this conference.

For information concerning the Faculty Recruitment Conference, the web site for that conference should be carefully read. That web site is:

http://www.aals.org/frs/

It is necessary to discuss some of the features of seeking a position while using the annual faculty recruitment conference. Before noting the details about the Faculty Recruitment Conference a few comments about timing the search for a full time position must be made. Law schools and universities generally, tend to do almost everything on the traditional academic calendar. School tends to start in the fall and maintain an active calendar until late spring. Recruitment of full time faculty members uses that same schedule. Law schools have their hiring committees begin to meet in early fall to consider the needs of the institution for the coming year. Resumes are considered in the fall and interviews take place by the end of the year or early in the next year. Offers are extended during the early part of the calendar year with the expectation that new faculty members will begin jobs the start of that following school year in the fall. The process, therefore, takes a full year. If a candidate is serious about seeking a full time law teaching position, that candidate should begin planning for that career change in the early summer of the year before that person actually wants to start that new teaching job. For example, if the candidate hopes to begin teaching in the fall of 2010, planning for that career change should begin in the summer of 2009. Obviously, if the candidate wants to add some features to the resume such as additional articles or an advanced degree, planning for the career change will have to begin much early.

Since law schools have a pattern and process that most of them follow, it will be necessary for candidates also to follow that pattern. If a candidate suddenly decides that he or she wants a teaching job that fall and starts sending out resumes in March, it is unlikely that any full time positions will be offered. Those will be offered to people who have been sending out resumes and talking with schools since the previous fall. Serious candidates for full time positions should closely follow the accepted pattern.

### 1. The Faculty Recruitment Conference

The Association of American Law School Faculty Recruitment Conference provides the best opportunity for finding a full time law school teaching position. Contacting the Association early and closely following the time periods indicated is necessary to take full advantage of the conference.

A candidate planning on participating in the conference should begin the process in the early summer. The Association should be contacted by visiting the web site noted above or writing for information. The web site can provide substantial information about how to participate in that conference.

The first major thing that the candidate for a position will want to do is prepare the brief resume for what is called the Faculty Appointments Register. After paying a fee, the candidate will be allowed to fill out a brief resume. That resume is then made available to law schools around the country. Almost all law schools that are interested in hiring will get access to that Faculty Appointments Register. The brief resumes that are supplied to law schools are distributed approximately four times during the hiring season. Those distributions begin fairly early in the fall. For that reason, candidates for positions should check the web site early, fill out the brief resume early and make sure that the process is begun early enough to be included within the first distribution. The earlier the resume is available to law schools, the more likely they are to see it and act on it.

The brief resume that is allowed to be provided will strike most candidates as very short. It is intended to be a brief overview of the candidate's basic credentials. It will, of course, ask for educational background, work experience, publications and other honors. An extra feature of this resume is that it allows the candidate to designate courses that are of interest for teaching. A candidate should think carefully while filling out that portion of the resume.

Filling out the section of the resume that allows a candidate to indicate courses that can be taught creates something of a dilemma. If the listing is too narrow or brief, a candidate may find that no law school in the country actually needs anyone in that area. A very limited or brief option of courses may exclude the candidate from any possible jobs. If, however, the candidate indicates that he or she is willing to teach anything in the curriculum that may look a little suspicious. Surely no one can teach every course in the curriculum. The candidate should clearly indicate the specific courses that are wanted. Then the candidate should also offer to teach a broader ranger of courses within that general area. If, for example, a candidate wants to teach and has experience in Real Estate Transactions, then Real Estate Transactions ought to be noted. A faculty member will probably have to teach four courses a year. No new faculty member will be allowed, however, to teach four sections of Real Estate Transactions. In addition, noting that the candidate could also be able to teach something like property would be important.

In making the list, candidates should remember that law schools all offer the basic courses in several different sections each year. Courses such as torts, property, contracts, civil procedure, Constitutional law, evidence, and corporations are always in great demand at law schools. A candidate that feels comfortable listing such courses will be open to more opportunities from hiring committees.

Tax law seems to be the one topic that does not quite fit that whole discussion. Law faculty members either teach tax or they do not. A faculty member that does not want to teach tax may freely say that tax is not an option. Such a candidate may be available during the first few years to teach almost anything but tax. For a candidate that wants to teach tax, that candidate may want to clearly state that tax is the first priority. For the candidate that wants to teach tax, however, there should be some thought given as to whether some other options are also available. Some law schools may need to add a tax professor, but won't be able to give the new person a whole schedule of tax. Being able to offer to teach tax and such courses as wills and trusts, for example, would be a good combination.

The suggested course offerings, therefore, is a difficult portion of the resume to fill out. The candidate will want to make the offerings as broad as the candidate feels comfortable suggesting. At the same time, the candidate wants to make sure that if a course is noted that it is possible for the candidate to make some intelligent comments about that topic if the interviewers begin to question about that topic.

The resume and interview process will also provide an opportunity to indicate a geographical preference for law schools. This is another topic that a candidate must carefully consider before entering the process. If the candidate narrowly limits where he or she is willing to locate, the opportunities for positions will also be limited. If, however, the candidate indicates that he or she is willing to take a position anywhere, that may lead to a waste of time and effort.

If there are clearly places in the United States where a candidate will not accept a position, then those locations ought to be noted. There is no reason to go through the process of interviews if the candidate knows that a position would be declined due to location. At the same time, candidates should look as broadly geographically as possible. There are, for example, numerous law schools in the northeastern portion of the United States and on the west coast. There are also a large number of candidates that indicate that they are unwilling to look any where except in the northeast or on the west coast. A candidate that narrowly limits the geographic preference to the northeast or west coast may be putting him or herself into the most competitive pool. Indicating a willing to move freely will open up more opportunities.

One additional note on the brief resume prepared for the Faculty Appointments Register. As with all resumes, make sure it is absolutely accurate. Any errors or even any appearances of errors will result in the candidate not being considered by most schools.

Once the brief resume is prepared, the candidate should also prepare a complete resume for his or her own use. Such a resume may be prepared and numerous copies run in order to be ready to provide prospective law schools with a more complete statement of the candidate's background.

In early fall, if the candidate has prepared the resume for the Faculty Appointments Register early enough, law schools will begin to review the resumes that are available. The candidate is not likely to hear from any law schools for a few months. During that period, the candidate may wish to mail out complete resumes to a few selected law schools of particular interest. Those resumes, together with a cover letter explaining an interest in a full time position, should be mailed to the Dean of the law schools. The Dean will forward such letters to a law school hiring committee. The hiring committees will spend most of their time reviewing resumes provided through the Faculty Appointments Register, but the addition of a full resume cannot hurt.

The actual Faculty Recruitment Conference is usually held in late October or early November. The web site for the Association of

American Law Schools should be checked to determine the exact date and time. Reservations for a room at the participating hotels should be made as early as possible for this conference. Almost all law schools will send representatives to attend the conference. Hundreds of candidates for faculty positions will also want to attend the conference. All of these people will be trying to get room reservations in the specified conference hotels. Finding a room for the conference can be extremely difficult if a candidate delays in seeking such a room. Just for ease and convenience during the conference, it is a great benefit to actually be in one of the conference hotels during the conference. It is important, therefore, to make the room reservation early.

Within a month of the conference, law schools will begin to call candidates and make appointments for interviews during the conference. Make sure that the contact information provided for the brief resume in the Faculty Appointments Register is accurate and supplies several telephone numbers. It would be unfortunate to lose a prospective position merely because the law school was unable to contact a candidate for an interview.

The interviews that are scheduled usually run for 30 minutes. The expectation is that law schools will be able to review resumes and conduct short screening interviews in order to see as many candidates as possible during the conference. Within a day or so of the conference, most law schools will have their whole interviewing schedule booked. Candidates should also have a good list of schools that they will be meeting. This is one of those times that candidates may need to think about the decision to go into law teaching. If, within a few days of the conference, a candidate has not gotten any calls to set up interview appointments, then there is actually no reason to go to the conference. It is rare that schools set up appointments once the conference has started. A candidate that goes to the conference with no interviews arranged will be lucky to get even one interview set up after arriving at the conference.

Upon arriving at the conference, it will probably be viewed as an unpleasant experience. There will be a few days of interviews with, hopefully, a multitude of law schools. There may be times when the candidate feels like all of the schools are starting to run together. To keep the schools from thinking that all of the candidates are running together, a candidate must approach the interviews seriously.

In approaching the interviews, candidates should bring multiple copies of a complete resume. Remember that schools will send more then one interviewer. Bring enough copies of a resume to be able to hand out several copies of the complete resume at each interview. If a candidate finds that copies of the complete resume are running low before the end of the conference, find a copy center and prepare more.

Upon entering an interview, keep in mind that this interview is a screening interview. A bad interview will result in losing any opportunity for the position. Try to keep the atmosphere pleasant but serious. Be prepared to talk about why teaching is an attractive career. In addition, interviewers may frequently ask about prior job experience or the nature of prior publications. If a topic appears on a resume, be prepared to discuss it.

Interviewers will frequently ask candidates if they have any questions. Since candidates get advanced notice as to who they will be interviewing, they should take a few minutes before the conference to look at the law schools' web sites. Note a few questions that could be asked about the school. Each school will probably have areas of special interest or special study. Ask a few questions about those topics. The screening interviews are not the time to ask about salary. That discussion can come much later.

After each interview, try to make a few notes to take home. After the conference, it will be difficult to remember everything that happened during those interviews. These notes might include the topics of discussion and the names of members of the interviewing team. There is just too much happening in too short of a period of time to remember very much of it later without notes. If a candidate is fortunate enough to get a call back interview from a school, it is nice to be able to comment on things that were discussed during the initial conference interview.

Also, after each brief interview and after making a few notes, try to completely forget that interview. It is possible that some of the brief interviews will not go well. If a candidate spends the rest of the conference dwelling on the bad interviews, that could have an impact on the performance in subsequent meetings. Take each interview as extremely important, conduct the best interview that is possible, and then forget it before the next interview.

The Faculty Recruitment Conference will have message boards available to all participants. Candidates should check the board regularly. A school may decide, after a good interview, to invite a candidate to a reception later. In addition, candidates may leave notes for schools that are attending the conference. If a school did not call a candidate for an interview, that candidate may leave a note and ask for an interview time. It is unlikely, however, that a school will grant such a request.

During the conference, there will be times when candidates are having quiet meals by themselves or attending receptions that are held. It should be remembered that the whole conference is a screening interview. A wonderful interview could easily be ruined by unfortunate behavior at a reception. Comments made during meals, in restaurants at the hotel, or during such receptions may be heard by people responsible for making decisions about call back interviews.

After the Faculty Recruitment Conference, law school hiring committees will return to their institutions in order to consider the candidates that they interviewed. During the period immediately after that conference, the hiring committees will select some of those candidates to be invited to the law school for a full day or two of interviewing with the whole law school community. The candidate should use this time to write a note to each of the hiring committees that was met during the conference. The note should thank the committee for the interview and then comment on some feature of the interview that was interesting. The letter can conclude by saying that the candidate looks forward to hearing from the school in the future.

A feature of participating in the Faculty Recruitment Conference is that the Association of American law Schools prepares a Placement Bulletin. This document is mailed out several times during the hiring season to all participants. It lists position openings that have been reported by schools. A candidate should look through that listing and mail a resume to schools that have listed jobs of interest.

Law schools do not make offers of teaching positions at the recruitment conference. That conference is intended to be used as a way to screen numerous candidates and then reduce the pool to three to six for any one position. Before offering a candidate a job, the school will invite that candidate to the law school for further interviews.

### 2. Invited to the School for an Interview

If the conference interviews were successful, the candidate will receive invitations to come to the law school for a full one or two day interview. Those interviews are usually scheduled before the end of December or, at the latest, in January. The law school will pay travel expenses and assist in the preparing the travel arrangements. This is another time that a candidate must realistically access the possibility of getting a full time teaching position. If no call back interviews are offered, the candidate may wish to reconsider the decision to go into full time teaching.

This call back interview is, for most schools, the final step in determining whether a full time position will be offered. This interview is, therefore, crucial to obtaining a position. Since the law school will be hosting the candidate, providing a hotel room and all meals, assume that the whole trip is an interview. As with the conference, it would be unfortunate for a great day of interviewing to be ruined by inappropriate behavior during dinner.

If a law school decides to offer a call back interview that means that the school is now serious about the candidate. The faculty members of the school will be asking questions to determine if the candidate is the best person for the position, but the faculty will also be trying to convince the candidate that the school is the best place for them. These campus visits can be informative and entertaining. Candidates should use them to make the best impression possible, but also learn more about legal education in general. Every campus interview will reveal many of the detailed aspects of the law teaching profession.

If a campus interview is extended, offer to send the hiring committee more copies of a full resume. That will allow the committee to distribute that resume to the rest of the faculty. In addition, bring copies of that full resume to the campus interview. If a candidate has reprints of past articles or other publications, it should be suggested that those can be mailed to the school also. Faculty members like to read prior publications.

The typical campus interview will have several features. The candidate will probably meet with the Dean or a Dean's representative. That discussion will offer some information about the law school generally. If given the opportunity, that conversation is a good time to ask about the school's tenure process and general salary range. The school will not be able to provide specific details at that moment about salary, but can offer some information.

During the course of the day, the candidate will meet with most of the faculty members. Those conversations will be as varied as the faculty themselves. Candidates will be asked about their writings and publications, reasons for wanting to teach, past work experience, and outside interests. Be prepared to talk about anything that appears on the resume.

Some schools may have faculty candidates speak to some students. It is difficult to know what students may ask. Be prepared to talk about expectations in the classroom and proposed teaching techniques.

A common feature of most campus visits is the requirement that the faculty candidate make a presentation to the faculty. This is an important feature of the campus visit for the candidate. A poor presentation sends several signals to the faculty. It may reflect an inability to do serious legal research and analysis, or it may reflect an inability to be a good pubic speaker. Either of those will result in the candidate not getting the job.

In selecting the topic for the presentation, a candidate should select one that the candidate knows well. Regardless of the nature of the topic, there will be a few faculty members that are somewhat knowledgeable about it. Those faculty members will follow the presentation closely and will ask questions. Gaps in knowledge will appear damaging.

Prepare well for the presentation. Try to pick a topic that will be of interest to a broad range of faculty members. Just because the candidate is an expert on a narrow tax regulation, does not mean that faculty members who teach everything but tax will enjoy it. Prepare a hand out or power point presentation. It is appropriate to ask the host for the campus visit if equipment will be available. If using a power point presentation, make sure it is a good one. It should be informative, helpful to the presentation, but not overly long. If planning on using power point or other technical features, make sure that the presentation can be made even if all of the technology fails. Go to the presentation assuming the worst case scenario.

In presenting the material, make sure it is accurate. A small error in a fact, or on a slide, will look horrible when faculty members have to decide about offering a job among several candidates.

After returning home from the campus visit, the candidate may want to write some notes to the specific host of the visit. That letter should comment on some interesting features of the visit and thank the host for the opportunity. Letters may also be written to the Dean of the law school and any specific faculty members that the candidate had particularly long or interesting conversations. The letters may end by noting that the candidate looks forward to hearing from the school in the future.

Sometime during the interviewing process, the school will check references on the candidate. The candidate would be wise to make sure that references that have been listed have been warned that the call may come. Some candidates like to avoid telling their current employers that they are seeking other jobs. It is possible to ask a law school to put off talking to a current employer until the last possible moment. After the campus interview, if the candidate is still being interviewed, the law school may then ask if it is possible to call the current employer.

### 3. The Offer

Law schools will be interviewing several candidates for any one opening that is available. The school will not be able to extend offers until all of the candidates asked to come to a campus visit have actually been to the school. For the early visitors, this may make it seem that the time between the campus visit and the offer is a long one. Most law schools will have completed all campus visits by the end of December or into January. Decisions will be made about offering positions and the offers extended in late January or early February. Schools like to make sure they have finished all of the hiring process by March.

Schools should notify candidates if they are no longer being considered for a position at that school. Schools should do that, but not all of them do. Some want to keep options open as long as possible in case the first or second choice of the school turns down the offers. If a candidate has not received some word by early March, there is still a possibility that the candidate is under consideration. That possibility, however, is weak. Most decisions will have been made by early March.

The offer will usually be initially extended by a telephone call from the Dean of the law school. (Again, make sure all contact information is up to date and correct.) That telephone call will probably be followed by a formal letter offer of employment. This is clearly the time to make sure all financial aspects of the position are clear. It is appropriate to ask about the full salary, tenure process, benefits, and even whether the school will pay for moving. It may also be a good time to ask if the school would pay for a return visit to the campus prior to making the final decision. The candidate may wish to look for available housing, allow a significant other to join in the decision making, or further review the life at the law school. Some schools will pay for such return visits; some schools will not.

Hopefully, a candidate will have several job offers from which to choose. If that is the case, selecting among the possibilities is much like choosing any job. The candidate should consider salary, location, courses that will be taught, tenure requirements, and other job details. There are also intangibles to consider. Law schools are groups of individuals who work together fairly closely. A job is more fun if the people get along well. If the people tend to argue and disagree, work can be difficult. If there are several job choices, consider all of the work environment features.

If there is only one job offer, the candidate must decide whether to take it. It is easier to move to another job in law teaching if the person already has a job in law teaching. Spending a few years showing success in the law teaching profession makes it possible to move to a position that may be more attractive. Keep in mind, however, that trying to be successful in a law school where the candidate is truly unhappy with the position is not going to be easy. A candidate will have to give serious thought about taking a job where only one is offered.

If no positions are offered, the candidate must again analyze the reasons for that. If there is something missing from the resume to make it strong enough to attract positions, the candidate may want to spend a few years strengthening the resume and then try again. If the whole process seemed to indicate that law teaching was not going to be available for the candidate in the future, then returning to the process for several years in a row may not be the best idea.

For the candidate that does not get an offer, but would still like to teach, thinking again of part time teaching is an option. That candidate can contact local law schools and inquire about being an adjunct.

# CHAPTER 3 - GETTING TO TENURE

It is generally thought that university teaching positions are the most secure jobs in the United States. Once a faculty member has earned the designation of being "tenured" that is probably true. After tenure, a faculty member may only be fired for narrowly defined reasons. Prior to tenure, however, university teaching may be the least secure job in the United States. That whole period before tenure is considered a probationary period.

Although the details of the tenure process are different in each law school, there are some clear similarities. The law school will have the full promotion and tenure procedure and requirements in writing. A new faculty member should get a copy of that document and read it closely. Early in the career, a new faculty member should talk with the Dean and make sure that all of the requirements of promotion and tenure are fully understood. It will be necessary for that new faculty member to closely follow those requirements in order to keep that job that took so long to get.

The general process of tenure is that a new faculty member is a probationary employee. Tenure is usually granted during a period of time specified by the law school or university. That period may be up to about seven years. During that period the new faculty member must demonstrate an acceptable level of competence in teaching, research, and service. If the new faculty member has not been granted tenure within the period specified by the law school, the new faculty member is usually fired. Full time faculty members are not allowed to remain on faculties as life-long untenured faculty.

It is important, therefore, for the faculty member to understand clearly the requirements and details of the tenure process. It is also important for the faculty member to take those requirements seriously. It is not uncommon for faculty members to be fired for failing to obtain tenure. This chapter will offer some help on how to meet those teaching, research, and service requirements.

### A. That Summer Before Starting the First Job

If everything goes appropriately, a candidate for a law teaching position will have finalized the acceptance of the job by mid to late March. That gives several months to close out any previous job commitments, housing issues, other details and begin the process of moving. Most of the issues to be confronted during the summer will be those that arise with any job relocation. Such typical issues will include finding new housing, getting use to a new city, and assisting any family with adjusting to a new city. There are, however, some special details to confront when moving to a new law school teaching job.

The law school will be finalizing the fall teaching schedule very soon after a new faculty member has agreed to join the faculty. Finding out what courses will be taught that fall should be a first concern. Someone in the Dean's office or on the faculty will be responsible for arranging that schedule and should be contacted promptly. That person will be able to give the names of the courses and, probably, the days and times of those courses. While getting that information, ask that person how one obtains complementary copies of course materials. All law book publishers will provide complementary copies of course materials that a faculty member may adopt. Someone within the law school will be able to explain the process and assist in obtaining those books. Try to have those books mailed as soon as possible. A new faculty member should have those books mailed to him or her personally in order to allow review of the books as early as possible.

While waiting for the packages of books to arrive, find out if there is someone on the faculty currently teaching additional sections of the same courses or if someone has taught those courses before. If that is true, call those people promptly. Explain that as a new faculty member, you will have to select course books and begin preparation. Ask if the faculty member has any advice. Most faculty members love to give advice. The experienced member of the faculty will probably recommend a primary, text, a secondary text, and any addition course materials. A truly helpful member of the faculty may also begin giving advice about how to present the course. Although new faculty members like to believe they can do it all without any help, getting assistance early on is important.

Once the packages of complementary books have arrived, the new faculty member should select books to use in the courses. It will be necessary to make sure that the university book store has time to order the books for your classes. Select the books early and contact the law school to make sure the book store orders the books.

As early as possible, begin to prepare for class. It is much more difficult and takes much longer to prepare for class than many new faculty members can imagine. Spending most of the summer getting ready for the fall classes is a great help to having a successful start to a new position. While preparing for those fall classes, do not forget that there will probably be another group of different courses to teach in the spring. A new faculty member should go ahead and be getting books to review for the spring courses as early as possible.

Upon moving into the new city, begin to visit the law school on a regular basis. Summer time is usually a slow period in law schools. Most of the faculty will not be in the building during mid to late summer and that makes it very easy to find one's way around. Try to get an office assignment and begin to get comfortable working in the new environment.

Many law teachers currently use one of the on line course management systems. Most universities have a system called Blackboard. In addition, both Westlaw and Lexis have their own versions of such systems. All of these systems allow a faculty member to place a syllabus on line, send messages to students, received messages from students, update material regularly, and generally manage the administrative details of the class. During the summer is an excellent time to start using one of the systems. This is another good opportunity to talk to other faculty members and the law school information technology people to determine which system most of the faculty uses. Once that decision is made, get help from those people to start setting up the on line pages for each of the classes.

Although preparing to teach those first classes should be the primary concern during that summer, some time should be spent thinking about research. If the new faculty member came from a graduate program, there are probably several topics that are almost completely researched already. If the new faculty member came from the practice of law, that faculty member should spend some time picking out two or three topics to consider. Once the school year starts, time will seem to move rapidly. It will be necessary to have substantial preparation for class and some preparation for research before that first day of class.

It may seem odd that much of the above material suggests getting started during the summer before the first class begins. Most law schools will probably not be paying a salary before school begins. It may seem that the new faculty member is working for the law school while not being paid. In fact a new faculty members who is coming from the practice of law, may prefer to continuing working with the old firm up until just a week or so before moving to the law school job. That would, of course, allow the new faculty member to avoid having any time where money is not being earned. Financial considerations may dictate that much of that first summer preparation is just not possible. A new faculty member must remember, however, that all of that preparation and work must be done sometime. Once classes begin, substantial time will be spent working with students. Some time will also be drained away working on committees and other service projects. Classes and research may suffer if preparation was not done earlier. Ultimately, the new faculty member will be judged on the quality of all of the work done. That must be considered when a new faculty member is deciding when to actually get started on class and research preparation.

### B. Find a Mentor

Once the first year starts, the new faculty member may assume that he or she is now working in that probationary period that leads up to the granting of tenure. It may seem that the time period specified by the law school is very long, but time has a way of moving rapidly. A new faculty member will have to prove competence in teaching, research and service if he or she hopes to be tenured. A dedication to accomplishing those goals is necessary. Each of those requirements will be discussed, but one item should be mentioned first. A new faculty member ought to find a mentor. In fact, a new faculty member ought to find several mentors.

The new faculty member will need to become proficient in teaching, research, and service. A good mentor from the current faculty that excels in those activities will almost be a necessity. If a new faculty member can find one person that excels in all of those areas that would be good. It is more likely that current faculty members will have a variety of strengths. The new faculty member will want to take advantage of the primary strengths of those different faculty members. In addition, working closely with several faculty members will aid the new faculty member to become a well known part of that faculty.

In selecting mentors, a few issues ought to be noted. First, try to find people who are well respected by other members of the faculty. There is no advantage to taking advice from someone that no one else respects. In addition, if there is a faculty member that seems to complain all of the time and is always discouraged, he or she would not make a good mentor. The mentors should be people who command the respect of others. Notice, for example, the conduct of other faculty members during faculty meetings. When a faculty member speaks, do the other members of the faculty tend to listen and accept what is said? That type of person would be a good mentor. If, however, the faculty member speaks and others tend to disregard what has been said, he or she would not make a good mentor. In addition, find mentors that respect privacy. There may be some faculty members that are successful in the law teaching profession, but also enjoy talking about what others have said to them. They may relay a new faculty member's questions or concerns to others. That type of person should be avoided with serious questions. There will be times when the new faculty member will need to ask questions that everyone else probably knows the answer to. A good mentor will answer it carefully and never mention it again.

Second, finding mentors within the same general subject area is a good idea. A new faculty member will be teaching classes and doing research. If there are current faculty members that teach and research in those areas, they may be able to provide good advice. Such mentors could suggest books for classes, methods of presentation of ideas, and general course organization. They could also provide topics for areas of research and a willingness to review early drafts of articles.

Third, it will be necessary to find a mentor that is respected as a good teacher. The early years of teaching in law school are difficult learning years. Law teachers are not required to have extensive training in the psychology of learning and most use teaching techniques that one of their own favorite teachers used. Many new law teachers find themselves struggling in the classroom. A senior successful teacher can provide tremendous insight into that area of the new work.

Fourth, a new faculty member should find a mentor that has a successful history of publications. New faculty members will be expected to research, write and publish. Some faculty members do this with ease, while others seem to struggle getting final projects into print. There are techniques for finding projects, completing those projects and seeing one's work into print. Find a mentor from among those who are successful.

Fifth, a mentor should be found that knows and understands the process to follow for promotion and tenure. The law school will have a written procedure for reaching those important goals. The law school will also have a common law or culture that has grown up over the years. A senior member of the faculty that has seen things go wrong in the past will be able to advise the new faculty member on how to navigate the promotion and tenure years.

Sixth, it would be a good idea to find some friends and companions that share common interests and backgrounds. These people will not be mentors, but may ultimately be friends. It is a worthwhile goal to find some colleagues close in age and life style. Having several colleagues of similar age and family style will provide people with whom shared experiences can be discussed. If a new faculty member feels that he or she is a member of a small group or minority, finding other similarly situated colleagues either on the law school faculty or on the university faculty may also be of some help. Such people will provide another resource for discussing shared experiences. Even when looking for friends to discuss the difficulties of the early years of teaching, remember to seek those who are successful and respected. Even within groups of newer faculty, there may be those who seem continually angry about events and conditions in the law school. Those people will not provide a positive atmosphere in which work can be completed.

It should now be obvious that a new faculty member will need a lot of help. Finding people already on the faculty that can provide that assistance will make the transition to successful law teacher much easier. If the law school provides a formal mentoring program, be sure and take advantage of it. Even if such a formal program exists, every new faculty member should also begin to build his or her own group of advisors and mentors.

### C. Work on the Teaching

In a few large, highly regarded research law schools, a poor teacher with an excellent record of scholarship can survive. That faculty member will be allowed to offer seminars to a narrow group of students as long as that faculty member continues to produce world changing scholarship. In most law schools, however, that will not occur. A faculty member must be able to teach classes. Not every faculty member will be the award winning, student favorite teacher. In most law schools, however, every faculty member must be able to command the respect of students and teach classes without major disasters.

Most law schools have several ways of measuring the quality of teaching. Generally, there is some combination of visits to classes by other faculty members, visits to classes by the dean and reviews of classes by the students in those classes. Each of those methods has its pros and cons.

Visits by other faculty members and the dean should produce a knowledgeable review. Experienced faculty members and the dean should be able to tell if the material is being offered in a sound and accurate manner. There are, however, problems with that method of review. Other faculty members and the dean ordinarily just review one or two classes out of a whole semester. If the faculty member being reviewed happened to have a particularly good or bad class, the reviewer would get a skewed view of what was occurring. In addition, researchers know that the presence of a viewer changes the conditions being viewed. That is certainly the case when another faculty member or dean walks into a classroom. The students in the classroom change behavior substantially. Some may try harder to look interested, while others will refuse to say a word.

Reviews of classes by students in the class are subject to debate within the legal teaching profession. There have been articles written which seek to point out the invalidity of such reviews. Many law schools find it necessary to constantly keep changing the survey form in an effort to get valid data.

Regardless of the techniques that the law school uses, the faculty will want to see that the new faculty member is doing a credible teaching job from the very first and is continuing to improve throughout the tenure process. Working with a mentor in this area will help the new faculty member to understand the expectations of the law school and improve the performance in the classroom.

i. Prepare and Prepare Again

One of the most important things that a new faculty member must learn about teaching is the importance of preparation. It may have been possible to skim material as a student, but that is not possible for the faculty member. An experienced trial lawyer coming into the classroom will realize that the preparation level is similar to preparing a case for trial. The difficulty will be that there are just not enough hours in the day to completely prepare.

The new faculty member must, of course, fully read, analyze and write up class notes for the book that was assigned to the students. That will include looking up all of the note cases and skimming all of the cited law review articles. The faculty member will then want to recommend some secondary sources for the students. Those will also have to be read closely.

Book editors and publishers do provide some helpful aids. Many of the casebooks will come with a "Teacher's Manual." Such a manual is not a substitute for full preparation. It may be helpful, however, to understand why the editor of the casebook included certain materials and the point that was trying to be made. At least during a first course preparation, the new faculty member should check on the availability of such a manual.

A law school teacher is not there merely to read the assigned text to the students. A good teacher will bring in a substantial amount of outside material to the classroom. Preparing enriching outside materials will also take substantial preparation time.

It must be understood that students will ask questions. The sign of a good class is that students raise issues and seek answers. In fact, student questions help the faculty member determine whether the class is able to understand the material. A series of good questions reflect a solid understanding the class. A series of strange or off point questions reflect that there is a problem. Substantial preparation will assist the new faculty member in being ready for such questions.

There will be times, however, when a student will ask a question that the new faculty member had not thought about before class. If the question is important, and the faculty member does not know the answer, then the faculty member must say that. Admitting that a question is a good one and that the faculty member will look for an answer before the next class is a reasonable way to respond. Students will be more respectful of an honest answer then they will of an attempt to deceive the class.

After years of teaching, I have noticed a trend about student questions. Such questions may fall into several types. Some questions are very good and must be answered clearly. Those questions may reflect that an important issue was not adequately covered or that some additional material must be brought to class. Those questions should be answered directly or by making a reference to other materials.

Some other questions generally flow from the discussion and merely offer the opportunity to further explain the material. Such questions may be additional fact patterns or special examples. A faculty member may spend as much or as little class time as seems appropriate to the level of interest of the class at large.

There are, however, some questions that are just off point. Students may be totally lost or just trying to waste a little class time. Those questions must be handled carefully. A faculty member does not want to waste class time with such questions. In addition, if time is spent on the questions, other students may start thinking that the issue is somehow important. The faculty member, therefore, needs to indicate that the question is not directly on point, and then move on. There has to be some care exercised in responding to such questions. In some classes, especially first year classes, students are having high degrees of anxiety. If a student asks a question and the faculty member announces, "That question is stupid and I'm not going to waste class time responding to it," the anxiety level goes way up. Other students will be afraid to ask any questions at all. They will become concerned that they may receive such an answer. The best response to time wasting questions is to say something like, "That question takes us a bit off of the material we're trying to cover today. If you want to talk about it some, come see me after class."

When a faculty member enters the class, the possibility of questions is one of the exciting things about teaching. It is especially exciting that there may be questions that were not thought about during the preparation process. After some years of teaching, I have noticed an additional thing about questions. Usually after I have taught a class for three years, I no longer get questions that I have not though about. It usually takes about three years to hear all of the questions. After that, any new question is probably not a good one.

### ii. Be On Time and Respectful

One of the topics discussed in the previous section addressed the importance of answering questions truthfully and respectfully. Treating the students with respect is an important feature in teaching. Law school faculty members are responsible to help educate the future lawyers of the United States. That includes providing a good role model in professionalism to those students. A faculty member should always maintain a professional, respectful attitude to students.

There was a time when legendary law professors were rude, abrupt, arrogant and insulting. Such professors seemed to delight in humiliating students. That time is over. There is nothing to be gained by such behavior. There is no doubt that the law professor knows substantially more about the material being covered then the students. In fact, with first year students, the law professor knows substantially more about the whole structure of the legal system then the students. It would be very easy for the law professor to embarrass and humiliate students. Even the mildest mannered professor can be pushed to the edge of such conduct when a student appears repeatedly unprepared. There is never a reason for such conduct. If a person is seeking a law teaching job because of the opportunity to engage in such conduct, then he or she should look elsewhere. There is no need for such people in the profession. In the modern world, such conduct will lead to loss of respect of students, loss of respect of the fellow faculty members and a real difficulty with gaining tenure.

Avoiding the attempts at humiliating students does not mean that the law teacher has to "go easy" on the students. The teaching profession, fellow law teachers and even the better students expect to be driven hard. The professor must set high expectations and question students in class in order to make sure those expectations are met. At the same time, students sometimes fail to be fully prepared for class. That may occur when a student has had a particularly troubling personal problem. It may occur when a student has tried to be prepared but failed to understand the material. Avoiding a lengthy classroom confrontation and moving on to a more prepared student is an easy way to avoid needlessly humiliating a student.

Finding the proper balance between high expectations and not humiliating students may seem difficult to the new faculty member. The key to the balance is to maintain a professional relationship with the students. Students should be expected to be prepared and display that preparation in class. Class discussion should be maintained on a high level. By use of good questions and positive leadership in the classroom, the faculty member can demonstrate those high expectations. If a student is consistently unprepared or engages in inappropriate conduct in class, that student should be told to visit with the professor after class. If the student is disruptive in class, that student should be asked to leave. Taking a firm but professional position in class will gain the respect of the students who are in the class to learn. Engaging in insulting or humiliating behavior will merely lose that respect.

Students pick up the signs of professional conduct and respect by many of the small things that a faculty member may do in class. When the faculty member makes sure that all aspects of the class are conducted properly, the respect of the students will be easily earned.

Faculty members believe that the time spent in the classroom is important. Students have differing attitudes about class activity. Some will never miss a class because they believe it is critical. Some will miss every class if allowed. In fact, some students will carefully select the courses they take based upon whether the faculty member checks attendance. It is up to the faculty member to demonstrate that he or she believes class is important. The behavior and conduct of the faculty member towards the class will serve as a role model of what the students believe about the class. As a new faculty member, it would be wise to consider the classroom experience important for the students.

In demonstrating that the class is important, the faculty member must be fully prepared for class. If the faculty member expects students to be prepared, then the faculty member can expect no less for him or herself. An earlier discussion in this chapter talked about the importance of preparation. That full preparation is a subtle message to the students that the faculty member believes what is happening the classroom is important. In addition to all of the other preparation, many successful classroom teachers add one additional step. For approximately one hour immediately before the class, those successful classroom teachers will set aside that time for a quiet period of reflection on the upcoming class. That time will be used to scan the material one more time, reflect on interesting questions that can be raised, or merely to remove all other issues from one's mind before the class. Full preparation and total focus on the class about to start will convince the students that class is important. It will also demonstrate a respect for the effort being shown by the students.

It is important for the faculty member to be on time to class. There are stories of the absent minded professor who shows up to class anywhere from one hour before class to 30 minutes late. The stories even tell of professors who forget a class is scheduled. Those stories may be interesting, but that behavior should be unacceptable in a law school. Showing up on time further demonstrates a commitment to the class activities. Successful faculty members may show up in the classroom approximately 10 minutes early. That allows time to open up notes and the book. It also provides time to set up any technology that will be used. It even allows the faculty member to erase the chalk board or white board and check for chalk or pens. By being a few minutes early, the faculty member can be standing in front of the class and ready to start at the appointed time.

The simple task of starting on time is another subtle device to accomplish many goals. It demonstrates to the students that the faculty member believes that class is important. It allows the faculty member to be ready to begin on time and fully use all of the time allowed for the class. It also makes it much easier to demand that students arrive on time.

As with starting on time, it is important to end on time. Students frequently have other classes. A class that runs over just a few minutes may make it difficult for the students to get to the next class. Keeping a class a few minutes late is also disrespectful to other faculty members. Another faculty member is probably using that same classroom for another class. There may be very little time allowed between classes. If one faculty member keeps a class over the time allowed, the next faculty member will be rushed in getting his or her class started. It is probably not in the best interest of an untenured faculty member to be delaying the start of a class being taught by a senior colleague.

As with start and stop times, it is important for the faculty member to hold the regularly scheduled number of classes when they are scheduled. There are clearly times when a faculty member may need to miss a class. Faculty members are human and may have personal issues. A faculty member may get sick or have a personal crisis in the family. Everyone will understand when those rare occasions arise. The faculty member must try to get word to the students that the class will be cancelled as soon as that information is known. Using email or web based course management systems allows the faculty member to notify all of the students promptly. The class time should be made up as soon as possible.

Faculty members should limit or avoid cancelling classes for other reasons. Faculty members have been known to cancel classes in order to engage in consulting or legal work, to travel or for other personal reasons. Such activity leads students to believe that class is not important in the eyes of the faculty member. It will also create concerns in the eyes of the rest of the faculty that the new, untenured member of the faculty may not be committed to teaching.

As with other cancellations, there are times when a faculty member will feel the need to reschedule classes for items that are less than emergencies. Some important conferences may be held during class times. The annual Association of American Law Schools conference for all law faculty members is, for example, held the first week of January. Some schools frequently find that part of the conference overlaps with the beginning of the January term of school. There are times when a faculty member may miss the first day or two of class in order to attend that conference. The reason for the absence should be explained to the students and the classes rescheduled.

Apart from law school teaching related reasons for being away from the school, some faculty members may decide to work outside the law school in consulting, lecturing or other activities. Such faculty members may frequently want to cancel and reschedule classes. Such activities create difficulties. Students come to believe that the faculty member is more concerned with outside activities rather than the class. Other faculty members become concerned about the commitment to teaching. All faculty members should avoid extensive time away from the classes. Untenured faculty members must absolutely avoid such time away. Frequent concerns about class attendance will create issues during the tenure process.

Student attendance in class is another issue that will have to be addressed by new faculty members. The American Bar Association in the accreditation requirements has a vague rule on monitoring regular class attendance. The vagueness allows schools to decide for themselves the best way to assure regular attendance by students. The methods used around the country are varied. Some schools will monitor attendance for the faculty member while others expect the faculty member to "take roll." Where the faculty member is expected to perform the task, there may be a variety of ways of assuring attendance. It may include having seating charts, passing a roll sheet for signatures, or even calling roll at the beginning of class. Some faculty members just do not bother with attendance. They may claim to spot check attendance or do some other random check method. Many of those, however, do not take roll. Students are aware of the process that faculty members use. If roll is not taken, some students will not attend. If roll is taken, attendance is higher.

The issue for the new faculty member is whether roll should be taken if the school is not directly monitoring that issue. From a practical side, the new faculty member should talk to successful mentors and find out what the general expectations of the faculty are. During the tenure process, the new faculty member would do well to appear to fit within the normal expectations of the institution.

Apart from the practical aspects of deciding a course of action, there are some benefits to monitoring attendance. When students notice that attendance is monitored, it again reflects a belief that class is important. Students may, at times, grumble about attendance, but will generally recognize it as an expectation. It also provides a way of monitoring student participation in class. There are times that a student will miss a few classes for personal reasons, and then feel anxious about returning. When a faculty member notices that a student has missed a couple of classes, it provides an easy excuse to contact the student and ask why. Students find it easier to maintain good performance in law school if the faculty notes their moments of difficulty and directs them towards appropriate assistance.

It would seem that with all of the emphasis on professionalism and respect, that the classroom would be a dull place. That is not necessarily true. Each faculty member is an individual and has his or her own personality. It is appropriate for faculty members to allow their personalities and individual interests to show through. It is even appropriate to find times for humor in the classroom. Students have anxieties and the occasional laugh will relieve the stress.

When using humor or deviating from the narrow discussion of the material, some care must be used. It is not appropriate to make a joke at a student's expense. It may seem funny at the time when a faculty member jokes or teases a student in front of the class. The student, however, is vulnerable and cannot respond. The student will feel attacked and forced to endure the laughs. Other students will also feel upset because they fear that they may be the next target of humor. It is never appropriate to carry the humor over into jokes about race, religion, gender, or ethnic background.

It is better to make jokes about oneself. For example, while the whole class struggles to understand a particularly difficult issue, jokes can be made by the faculty member about how many times he or she got confused on the issue. Finding a way to express one's own humanity is permissible in the classroom.

In taking short deviations from the clear points of the class, faculty members must remember the importance of maintaining reasonable behavior. There is nothing gained by wasting large amounts of time on some unimportant story. Students will notice, but not appreciate, such waste of time. Telling long, absurd stories or engaging in strange behavior is contrary to maintaining the professional, respectful attitude to students.

One final issue should be noted before leaving the topic of preparation and respect to students. New faculty will have to decide what to wear to work and, especially, class. One remembers mythical university professors wearing tweed sport coats with patches on the elbows. Many of such myths also included pipe smoking. Whether such myths were ever true is questionable; they are clearly not true now. University professors in general and law school professors in particular dress in a variety of different ways.

Law school professors tend to dress a bit more conservatively then university professors at large. One is more likely to see dark professional suits on both men and women law professors then in other units on a university campus. Within a single law school, a new faculty member may find a variety of manners of dress. Some faculty members will look like they are getting ready to go to a courtroom for litigation. Such men and women faculty members will be regularly dressed in dark, professionals suits. At the other end of the spectrum, some faculty members will be dressed casually. Such men and women faculty members will be dressed in jeans and t-shirts. Between those extremes a new faculty member will see faculty members wearing sweaters, sport coats, light jackets, sport shirts and blouses, khakis, and a variety of other clothing styles. Once a faculty member reaches tenure, he or she can probably wear whatever seems appropriate. Prior to tenure, a little care should be exercised.

As with all issues in a law school, there is probably a common law culture on appropriate dress for school. This is another place that a new faculty member may look to senior mentors for guidance. It is probably not even necessary to ask a question. Notice what the successful and respected members of the faculty are wearing. Do not drift too far from that trend. A new faculty member is not going to be denied tenured for inappropriate dress. It is not necessary, however, to create an issue where one can be so easily avoided.

There is one interesting point about appropriate attire in the classroom. When students are interviewing for legal jobs or actually work part time in a law office, those students will begin to show up for class in professional attire. The students realize that they are required to wear dark professional suits in the law setting. Many successful faculty members use that subtle piece of information as another way to create the professional atmosphere in the classroom. By wearing professional attire to class, the faculty member becomes a role model for the students. The class takes on one more aspect of the future the students face in the practice of law.

### iii. Relationship to Students

Throughout the previous section, the overriding theme was to create a professional, respectful relationship with students. That relationship must carry over to contact outside of the classroom. The teaching aspect of the job does not end when the class time is over. Students will come to the faculty member's office or stop the faculty member in the hallway to ask questions. There are even times when the student will see the faculty member in the city away from the school. It is important to remember that the faculty-student relationship will exist for as long as that student is enrolled in the law school. It is funny, but many students continue to feel that faculty-student relationship long after graduation. Senior faculty members are pleased to hear members of legislatures and appellate courts who were once students still use the term "professor" when they are seen out in public. Many well known, successful lawyers still show great deference to faculty members they had in law school.

Some students will try to be "friends" with faculty members. There may be a variety of reasons for that. Students have anxieties and may want a more personal relationship to solve that problem. Some may being trying to avoid the issue that the faculty as a whole will be deciding class rank and whether graduation even occurs. Others may just try to make friends with everyone. If a faculty member gets too friendly with students, it makes the grading and other judging issues of the job much more difficult. Students will expect some leniency based on the friendship. Other students will suspect unfair treatment because they were unable to form such ties. In the way that lawyers must maintain a professional relationship with clients, faculty members should strive to that end.

New faculty members may find themselves in a particularly difficult position. The new faculty member may be closer in age to most of the students then to many of the other faculty members. That new faculty member may find going to bars and having a few drinks with a variety of students to be preferred to having dinner with a senior colleague. Drifting into socializing with students on a regular basis, however, is not in the best interest of the new faculty member's career. The expectations of the students may change because of that close contact. Even worse, the students may object to the faculty member following along. Being students, however, they will not be able to figure out how to tell one of their teachers that they are not wanted. Such conduct should be avoided.

Being professional, however, does not mean being "remote." Faculty members must be available to answer questions and give direction to students. Students also like to see faculty members engaged in a wide range of school activities. Supporting different students groups is seen as a positive faculty activity. Students, for example, will frequently have official student functions. Those might include law school fraternity events, orientation week events, student graduation events, or other such activities. A faculty member should feel comfortable attending one or two such events. Faculty members may even be asked to be a "faculty advisor" to certain student groups. Discussing those events with a respected faculty mentor can provide some guidance on the typical and expected behavior of the faculty as a whole.

One issue of faculty-student relationships is difficult to discuss, but must be addressed. The issue is intimate relationships between a faculty member and a student. In times past, the typical law school faculty was all or predominantly male. During those periods, there were times when a male faculty member would engage in a sexual relationship with a female student. It is likely that such conduct continues to occur. As more women have joined law school faculties and a broader acceptance of differing sexual preference has occurred, the issue may expand. Women faculty members may have such relationships with male students and faculty members of both genders may have same sex relationships with students.

When such relationships arose in years past, they were usually quietly dealt with. The parties to the relationship would resolve the issue and the institution would usually try to ignore it. That was not a good solution and would clearly not be the solution today.

Some people will seek to defend the right to engage in such relationships. They will note that all law students are of adult age and have the right to consent to such conduct. They will further claim that if the parties mutually consent to such conduct then the privacy of the individuals demand that no one else has the right to interfere. Even such defenders will admit that the faculty member must be careful not to create a conflict of interest. If, for example, the faculty member is having a sexual relationship with a student who will receive a grade from that faculty member, there is a problem. The student in the relationship will be favored, and other students will feel at risk for lower grades.

Most other people, including me, will feel that a sexual relationship between a faculty member and a student is always wrong. That wrong is on the part of the faculty member. The reason for that opinion is that many people believe that the faculty member is in a position of real or apparent authority. That authority is over the student with whom the faculty member is having the relationship. Even if the student is not in a class with that faculty member during the duration of the relationship, the position of the faculty member in the law school gives the faculty member substantial authority over the student. Because of that power there is no real "consent" on the part of the student to the relationship. In addition, the conflict of interest exists and cannot be eliminated.

For those who still wish to defend the right of faculty and students to have intimate relationships, there is a practical reason to avoid the problem. Law schools have recognized some exposure to liability for claims of sexual harassment. Most schools have lengthy sexual harassment policies and require all employees to undergo sexual harassment training. If a law school is threatened with a claim of sexual harassment, that school will not be sympathetic to a faculty member having a sexual relationship with a student.

If a relationship ends badly, the student may have one of two claims for sexual harassment. The student may claim that sex was demanded in return for grades and make the claim in the nature of a "quid pro quo" claim. In the alternative, the student in the relationship or even other students may allege that the atmosphere around the faculty member was so sexually active as to create a hostile environment.

In short, the best advice concerning the issue of sexual relationships with students is to avoid such conduct completely. The relationship will be damaging to the school and may lead to termination of employment.

### iv. Teaching Techniques

In all of the discussion about teaching, there has been nothing said about teaching techniques. There is not one perfect system of presenting the material in class. Law teachers usually do not have an educational background, or training in the psychology of teaching. This means that law teachers usually do not have real skills in selecting good teaching techniques. Most law teachers seem to recall what methods they saw as students and try to use those methods that are remembered as successful. The difficulty with that procedure is that it has many flaws.

First, the law teacher may not accurately remember what techniques were actually used in the past. The faulty memory may result in the new law teacher believing he or she is using some traditional technique when that is wrong. In addition, the new law teacher may have had a way of learning that was and remains different from most students. Something that worked for that one person may be a complete failure for all other students. New law teachers should take some time to think about appropriate teaching techniques.

It should be noted that the idea of showing respect for students reenters the discussion when considering teaching techniques. The traditional idea that law teachers should be rude and arrogant is no longer acceptable. The role of the law teacher is to help prepare the students for a profession. Using humiliation as a technique is wrong.

A first step in considering proper techniques is to gain some information about teaching. The Association of American Law Schools offers annual conferences for new law teachers. Those conferences are usually offered in the summer and provide a good overview of what it takes to be a successful law teacher. A new law teacher should ask his or her new Dean if funding is available to allow attendance at that conference. The conference is expensive and that may make it difficult to attend without law school support.

There are, of course, other avenues to gain information about teaching techniques. As with all other issues in a law school, a new teacher should seek the advice of mentors. There will be faculty members in every law school who are recognized as successful teachers. Talk to those faculty members about the techniques that they use. If scheduling permits, ask those faculty members if it is permissible to sit in on a few of their classes. Most senior faculty members would be delighted to know that a new teacher wants to "learn from the master." Observing successful techniques is one of the best ways to understand what works.

It is also useful to read books on the psychology of learning. A university library will have a wealth of books on that topic. A brief stop in the university library will allow the new teacher to find several books that can provide a background for improving teaching. Of course, if the new teacher can make the acquaintance of a professor in a department of education, that acquaintance may be able to recommend a few sources.

Keep in mind that, in a law school setting, most of the students will be learning through two different senses. They will be learning through vision and hearing. Teaching materials and teaching techniques should offer information through both of those senses.

Traditional classes offered materials for both sight and sound. The books would allow the student to gain information visually. Discussions with other students and discussions in class would offer information through sound. Using both of those allows the student to reinforce the learning that is gained through each.

Recent years have seen a major change in technology in schools and colleges. Most law students had computers in undergraduate school and now own their own laptops. Having used such equipment throughout college, those students expect to continue to use it in law schools. The students will use the laptops to take notes in class, schedule meetings, check email, and do research. Modern students have also adapted to using audio technology. Most law students have cell phones and mp3 players. The most common mp3 player is, of course, the iPod. A faculty member that fails to take advantage of that technology is missing an opportunity.

Universities and law schools now provide computer based course management systems. Both Lexis and Westlaw have such systems. Most universities also use a system that is called "Blackboard." Those systems allow the professor to post assignments, set schedules, post additional materials, manage class rolls, and generally do all of those things that use to be done on paper. A new faculty member should find out which of the systems that most of the faculty use and use that one. By using the system that most of the other faculty use, it will make it easier to get help in learning the system, and it will be easier for the students to learn only one system.

Most people are now familiar with a computer based program called "Power Point." That software allows the teacher to make and display slides to an audience. A "Power Point" slide show to accompany a class does provide some advantages in certain ways. Where there are materials that the whole class needs to view at once, for example, a slide with that information is helpful. New teachers should be careful when using "Power Point." If the new teacher makes up multiple slides for every class and becomes tied to a presentation that cannot be changed, class may become stilted and routine. The law professor must be able to move and change the class based upon the issues raised during class discussion.

Many law schools are providing updated facilities in the classroom that allow use of modern technology during class. Sometimes referred to as a "smart board" or "smart podium" the equipment can be used to present and preserve a variety of materials in modern form. A new faculty member should inspect the classrooms at the earliest opportunity. If the classrooms have the new technology, that new faculty member should seek out help form the law school's technology staff to gain an understanding of how the equipment works.

There is national technology organization or cooperative of law schools in which all schools participate. This organization is the Center for Computer Assisted Legal Instruction. It is routinely referred by its acronym of "CALI." For complete information about CALI, see their web site at:

http://www2.cali.org

CALI provides supplemental lessons that can be used for most classes. In addition, CALI provides audio podcasts of lectures and discussions. The organization can be used without charge by all faculty members of member schools. Such faculty members may suggest or assign computer lessons and podcasts. They may also create their own lessons or podcasts for student use. CALI also provides a site for faculty members to create their own blogs. Students can download lessons to their own computers, read the faculty member's blog, and even download podcasts to mp3 players. CALI is currently working on creating and storing teaching and class materials for use by law teachers. For additional education and training in using computer technology in law school, CALI also hosts an annual conference each summer. That conference offers workshops on the full range of issues that arise with law schools and computers. Information about the conference is available on the website.

At some point, a new law teacher will have to confront the issue of whether to use lecture or class discussion. In law schools, the class discussion is usually referred to as the "Socratic Method." Most law teachers find that they use some combination of both. There are times when a little lecture helps introduce some material or recap things already covered. If a class is completely lost on a topic, a short lecture will help clear up some confusion. Most law teachers find, however, that lecturing for all of the class time is not productive.

Encouraging the students to participate in the class discussion is helpful for several reasons. Having the students talk and explain material helps the students to learn the basic material. That student discussion also helps students to learn to speak and articulate ideas in public. The student discussion will also assist the faculty member in determining whether the students understand the material. Finally, student discussion breaks up the time spent in class. Few speakers, even law teachers, are able to lecture for the full class time and remain interesting. Nothing but lecture has a tendency to lose the students. Using some type of class discussion helps maintain the student interest in the material.

The actual method of presentation of the material will be partially dependent on the teaching materials selected. If, for example, a new faculty member uses a traditional case book, some form of case analysis will be used. If that faculty member selects a problem book, then discussions of problems will be the norm. As a new faculty member's skill and experience increases, that faculty member may find it useful to use a mixture of cases, statutes, problems, text materials, computer lessons, podcasts, and blogs. Using a variety will allow the students to use both visual and auditory learning while keeping the students from getting board with a tedious routine.

One additional source for law teaching help must be noted. Gonzaga University School of Law has an "Institute for Law School Teaching." This institute offers on-line materials, publications and a newsletter. Access to these materials may be obtained by using the Gonzaga University School of Law website at:

http://www.law.gonzaga.edu/About-Gonzaga-Law/Institute-for-Law-School-Teaching/default.asp

v. Preparing the Exam

Law schools have a tradition of only having one exam for each course. That exam comes at the end of the course as a final exam. This results in the one exam controlling the final grade in the class.

Many law teachers have become concerned that having only one exam for a course is not in the best interest of the students. Those law teachers are starting to use mid-term exams, additional papers and even a few pop quizzes during the course of the semester. A new faculty member should talk to mentors about usual expectations at the law school. As a new faculty member, it would probably be unwise to differ very much from the usual practices. After some years of experience, that would be the time to begin to experiment with different testing techniques. Since the major portion of most courses will be the final exam, some time should be given to discussing the preparation of that exam.

The new faculty member should begin working on that final exam very early. As each section of material is covered during the semester, the faculty member can make some brief notes about possible areas for questions. By the time the semester is one-half to two-thirds over, the process of writing the exam should begin in earnest. It is also about this time in the semester that the new faculty member should talk to mentors to find out if there are any special features of exam preparation that should be known. Some schools, for example, may require faculty members to turn in finished exams to a staff office by a certain date. Other law schools may require faculty members to do most exam preparation. Knowing the law school practice and meeting those requirements on time will make sure that the new faculty member does not offend colleagues.

In preparing the exam, the new faculty member may want to take a look at old exams by other faculty members. If, for example, a respected member of the faculty has been teaching in the same area for some time, there are probably old exams on reserve within the law school. The new faculty member can look at those exams to get some idea of length, level of difficulty, and general format. The new faculty member should not, however, borrow questions from those old exams. Students will have the same access to those old exams. The faculty member who prepared the old exam will feel that something inappropriate was done if questions are borrowed. It is, however, permissible to view the old exams to get some idea of format. If old exams are not generally available, talk to mentors and ask to borrow copies of old exams. After explaining why the old exams want to be viewed, most senior faculty members will be delighted in sharing their previous work.

Law school exams are traditionally set up as long essay or problem questions. Such exams have been the staple of law schools for years. Some faculty members have begun to use some short answer and objective questions on some exams. New faculty members usually find it easier to draft problem questions when working on that first set of exams. Objective questions are difficult to prepare. Essay or problem questions can open up the course to a broad discussion and then allow the faculty member to grade based upon the answers received.

After a draft of the exam is prepared, the new faculty member should ask a senior mentor to read over it. Obviously, this works best if that mentor teaches in the same area. Having someone review the exam accomplishes several goals. The reviewer will be able to note any clear grammar or typographical errors. In addition, the reviewer will notice any problems with confusion over names or parties, identity of issues or other logic difficulties. Finally, a senior mentor will be able to get a sense of whether the exam is appropriate for the class. That reviewer may note that an exam is too easy or too hard.

In giving the exam, the new faculty member will have to ask mentors about the practice of the law school in giving exams. Some law schools expect the faculty member to administer and proctor his or her own exams. Other law schools expect the faculty member to be out of the building, and exams are administered by staff or students. In addition, law schools differ on how, where, and when grades are to be turned in. A few casual conversations with mentors can provide information that will help the new faculty member avoid being out of line on the procedure.

Once the exams have been given, the new faculty member will have to grade them. As noted earlier in this book, grading exams is the hardest part of the law professor's job. It must be completed in a reasonable period of time and futures of individual students depend on the outcome of that grading. Grading must be done with absolute seriousness.

Before finishing up the grading of exams, a new faculty member should talk to senior mentors about the usual grade expectations. A new faculty member will find that it is easy to arrange the papers in a descending order of quality. It is easy to put the best paper on top and arrange the rest in descending quality until reaching the worst paper. The difficult part of grading is deciding where those papers fall on the grading scale. If, for example, the law school uses a tradition "A,B,C,D,F" scale, such grades must be awarded to the papers. The new faculty member will need some guidance to know what the usual expectations are about grades.

Some law schools use a mandatory or suggested curve. If that is the practice, it will be necessary for the new faculty member to fit the papers within that curve. Other law schools may not have a formal curve, but there will be a generally known expectation about grades. If, for example, a school usually finds that most courses fall into a "B minus" curve and the new faculty member's classes are substantially out of line, there will be difficulties for the new faculty member. Students will be upset and the Dean will have to talk to the new teacher. All of that can be avoided by talking to a few mentors prior to turning in grades.

After the grades are revealed to students, the cultures of law schools differ as to whether students have the opportunity to review and discuss the papers. Some law schools seem to create road blocks to students wishing to discuss exams. Other law schools encourage students to go to professors and discuss performance. A new faculty member should follow the lead of the law school culture on that issue.

If the law school encourages discussion about grades, a new law teacher will find those discussions can be difficult. Some students with high grades will want to look at exams just to enjoy the moment. Other students will be unhappy with grades and want to complain. New law teachers will even find some students sitting in the office crying over low grades. Through out the process, the new law teacher must maintain a calm, professional approach to the discussion. The grades earned in law school are of utmost importance to the students. Although the faculty member does not feel that grades are "personal," students seem to take the grades very "personally."

During the grade discussion process, a new faculty member will be surprised to learn that some students will ask to have grades changed. The question may come in a variety of different ways. A student may ask that the papers be "regraded." Some students will want to go over the papers for a long period of time hoping to find a "few points." A few may just ask that the grade be raised since it causes the student some harm. If a few grades are changed, the faculty member will get a reputation for changing grades. That reputation will go through the student body in a very short period of time, and the faculty member will spend the rest of his or her career dealing with changing grades. That is a reputation that a faculty member does not want.

In grading the papers, it is important to be extremely careful. Make sure that each paper is graded with a grade that can be defended. An accurate grading of the papers will take an extremely long time. It will, however, be time well spent. It is useful to have a grade sheet or answer sheet that can be referred to in explaining the shortcomings of any paper. The papers should then be compared to each other to make sure that each grade is consistent with those of the other students. Before turning in the grades, carefully recheck the math or computation that generated the grades. A simple math error can result in wrong grades being award to whole groups of papers. Nothing can be more frustrating or embarrassing then having to change multiple grades due to a simple math error. Once the faculty member is certain that the grade is accurate, there should be no reason to change it.

There are, of course, times when a mistake can happen. Math errors, errors in reporting the grade, or other procedural error may occur in getting the final grade posted. If that occurs, it may be necessary to correct the grade. Each law school will have a procedure for making such corrections. It will be necessary to check with mentors or law school records staff to determine the proper way to correct grades.

Although law schools have a method of correcting grades once an error has been found, a new faculty member does not want to be seen as constantly having to correct grade errors. Such a practice will lead the senior faculty to assume one of two possible reasons. The senior faculty will assume that the new faculty member is either careless with grading or changing grades because students complain. Neither assumption is a good one.

### D. Getting the Research Published

Once the classes are moving forward, the new faculty member will have to begin thinking about research. Publish or perish has become the rule in law schools. If a new faculty member does not do adequate research and publications, that faculty member will not be tenured. Failure to earn tenure means that the faculty member is not allowed to stay on the faculty. In short, the faculty member will be fired. It is necessary, therefore, to take the research requirement seriously.

There are still those in legal education that view the research requirement as a meaningless hurdle that new faculty members have to clear. It is a viewed as something to require of new faculty members, but not to be taken seriously. The number of people in legal education that think that way is small and getting smaller. Most law professors feel that research and publications are an important part of the law teacher's job. The research and publications allow the professor to create new ideas and share them with the public. The research also allows the teacher to continue to educate him or herself in order to improve the classroom experience for students.

Most law schools will have a written document that outlines the promotion and tenure rules. That document should state the expectations for research and publications. After carefully reading that document, the new faculty member should have a meeting with the Dean to analyze exactly what is expected in terms of type of research and quantity of research. The new faculty member should also talk to mentors about the usual expectations. Mentors can discuss exactly what the new faculty member must do. Deans and faculty members will not be sympathetic to a person coming up for tenure who claims that he or she did not know what was expected.

i. Types of Research?

There has always been some continuing dialog about the appropriate type of research that should be completed by new, untenured faculty. The traditional distinction was between law review articles and books. Although a few law schools may have thought that every tenured professor needed at least one hard back publication, most law schools expected traditional law review articles to be the norm. Modern technology has expanded the debate. There is a current discussion about the roll of self published books and blogs in the tenure decision. When books, law review articles, self published books and blogs are added to newspaper articles, bar association magazines and any number of other possibilities, the new faculty member may feel that the possibilities are endless. For a safe path to tenure, the possibilities can be narrowed.

Most law schools would recognize the need to publish traditional law review articles. A new law faculty member should assume that research and publications during the pre-tenure period will focus on those traditional articles. There may be opportunities to work on books or other types of projects, but they should be viewed as extras. The goal of reaching tenure should rely on the traditional articles.

Most law schools have become concerned with the appropriate law journal in which articles should be placed. Law school deans may be heard to talk about placing articles in the top 25 or top 50 law journals. Obviously, that raises the difficulty of placing articles. If, however, the law school seems to be moving in that direction, the new faculty member will have to try to meet those goals.

In preparing the research and publications, the new faculty member may have opportunities to co-author works. Accepting such an opportunity may have its problems. Many senior faculty members will be unwilling to recognize co-authored works as true tenure reviewing material. There is a concern that it is difficult to tell who actually did the work on a co-authored piece. In reviewing a faculty member for tenure, the senior faculty will want to see what the new faculty member can do. Falling into a co-author project can also be time consuming. A new faculty member may accept a co-author assignment only to find that the other authors are expecting the new faculty member to do it all. It would be unfortunate to have to do all the work and then fail to get any credit during the tenure process. Of course, some co-author projects may work to a new faculty member's advantage. If a new faculty member was asked to co-author a work with a nationally known scholar, that connection would advance the career of the new faculty member. In short, co-authoring should not be seen as a step towards tenure. The new faculty member should expect that only sole authored works will be reviewed and accepted for tenure. If a great co-authoring opportunity arises, the new faculty member can participate while doing other necessary publications.

### ii. Doing the Research and Completing the Projects

New faculty members will find that doing the research and completing the projects are difficult. Classes are scheduled and must be met at specific times. Preparing for those classes will become time consuming. Committee work and faculty meetings are usually scheduled and will be done at specific times. The faculty member must also set aside a certain number of hours a week for "office hours." After class preparation, teaching, office hours, and committee work, the new faculty member will feel like going home and doing nothing. Other time that is available during the day will be spent checking email, checking voice mail, looking at "snail mail," drinking coffee, and talking to colleagues. The easiest thing to avoid doing is the research. Many faculty members fall into the trap of assuming that they will work on the projects "in the future." There is usually not a specific deadline for research other then the tenure date which is six or seven years in the future. Many faculty members will decide that they will wait until they have a nice long period of uninterrupted time to work on a project before getting started. Because of class preparation, teaching, and committee work, the long period of uninterrupted time never appears. Those faculty members seem to always be busy but never complete a research project. If an untenured faculty member follows that pattern, he or she will lose the job at the tenure review date. In fact, without substantial work being done on a regular basis during the six or seven years leading up to the tenure date, the faculty member may lose the job even earlier. Time must be found to do the research and writing.

It was noted in the previous paragraph that classes, office hours, committee meetings and faculty meetings are scheduled. A new faculty member should schedule time for research. It is a common fallacy that a faculty member needs long, uninterrupted time for research. With computer assisted legal research through Lexis or West, research can be done in the office in short bursts of time. A faculty member should set aside 30 minutes to an hour each day for research and writing. Just as all other activities are scheduled, the research can be scheduled. It is not necessary to announce that portion of the schedule, but it can be accomplished. The faculty member can close the office door or go to the library for that scheduled period. It does not have to be at the same time every day. Due to class and committee meetings, research may be scheduled at different times each day. During different times of the year, the length of time scheduled each day may differ. Developing a regular, routine schedule of research and writing, however, is the best way to make sure the job is completed. Within a few months of such scheduling, the new faculty member will discover that the research and writing is as much a part of the daily work as teaching, class preparation, and committee meetings.

Once the time for research is found, it is time to get started. The first task is finding a topic. For those coming from a graduate program, use the masters thesis or some class paper as a good place to start. For those coming from practice, start on the big issue that is current in that area of practice. For both, there are probably topics within the classes being taught that just beg to be studied. There are an abundance of issues to research for anyone entering the teaching profession. As an aid to finding topics, get a small notebook and start writing down topic ideas on individual pages. Use a new page for each idea. When the idea presents itself, write down a sentence or two on the idea at the top of a page. During quiet moments, add detail to each of those pages to help expand the idea. If some good source materials, cases, statutes or articles are found that that could be used to begin researching a topic, add it to the page that concerns that topic. Within a short period of time, the new faculty member will have a current topic to research together with a notebook full of future topics to research.

It is beyond the scope of this book to tell any new law teacher how to research and write a law review article. Those techniques should have been developed earlier. The main purpose of this work is to encourage the new faculty member to continue working on the topic on a daily basis. The project will not finish itself. It will require constant attention.

iii. Placement of Articles

The traditional method of placing an article is to mail copies of the article to selected law schools until one decided to accept it for publication. That technique may still be used and produce results. The new faculty member will want to select a list of possible law reviews and then begin mailing out copies. Some law reviews want to be the only one reviewing the article at one time, so only one should be sent at a time. It would be appropriate to ask the law review to contact the author within a specified period of time in order to make sure the process does not take to long.

A modern approach to placement of articles is to use the internet. The Social Science Research Network (SSRN) provides a web site for posting information about articles available for publication. A new faculty member should check with mentors and the law schools technology staff to determine whether the law school is using that service. If so, mentors and the staff will assist the new faculty member in placing abstracts of completed work on the internet. This can expedite placement of articles.

iv. Talk to Mentors

Throughout the research and writing process, talk to mentors. There will be successful researchers on one's own faculty. Talk to them about getting started, possible topics, and completing the projects. Also seek advice on placement of the article. It would also be useful to ask trusted mentors to read and comment on articles. When suggestions and recommendations are made, incorporate them into the article.

In addition to in-house mentors, seek mentors in other law schools. Teachers or advisors from one's own past or noted scholars in the area are frequently willing to read and comment on new faculty member's work. Incorporate their suggestions and comments into the article.

v. Conferences

Attendance at conferences is a good way to gain ideas for future topics and to make presentations of current research. Although it is difficult for new faculty member to get on programs, regular attendance at conferences will help produce such invitations.

Some conferences actually provide specific opportunities for young scholars to make presentations. The Southeastern Association of Law Schools, for example, holds a conference each summer. In addition to regular sessions and workshops, the conference sets aside times for presentations by young scholars. If located in the southeast, it would be a good opportunity to ask the Dean to send a new faculty member to that conference for the purpose of making such a presentation. For information about the conference, see their web site at:

http://www.nsulaw.nova.edu/seals/

### E. Doing the Service

Universities as a whole and law schools in particular will expect faculty members to render service. Service is a broad concept that encompasses many activities. It ranges from participating in faculty governance in the institution to performing some pro bono work in the community. The goal of each new faculty member should be to find a balance among law school service, university service and service to the profession.

i. Faculty Meetings

Faculties at all institutions have faculty meetings. These meetings may be held monthly, weekly, or even more often when needed. The faculty meeting is where all of the decisions of the law school should be made.

For those in private enterprise, it seems odd that a faculty should have so much control over the direction of the institution. Educational institutions, however, are not run "like a business." Educational institutions are designed to educate and create new research. Those doing the educating and research are in the best position to know how that work should be done. Because of that understanding, there is a delicate split of authority between faculties and administrators. An easy way to visualize the split is to recognize the faculty as the legislative body of the law school while the dean is the executive.

Educational institutions also have Boards which oversee the whole operation. Because of the existence of a board, everything done by the dean and faculty must come within the authority granted by that Board. During periods of relative calm, the Boards may let the faculty and dean work without much guidance. During periods of crisis, such as financial difficulties, the Boards may take a more active part. Faculty meetings during periods of relative calm can still be time consuming.

Faculty meetings may routinely review curriculum, admissions, research expectations or any of a number of other recurring issues. Such faculty meetings will require the attendance by all faculty members. Faculty committees will have prepared initial materials and respond to questions by the faculty.

Attendance and participation at faculty meetings are expected parts of law school service by all faculty members. A new faculty member must attend all faculty meetings and be prepared to listen carefully to what is said. Much of the history and culture of a law school can be determined by noting the discussions in such meetings.

Some new faculty members will have an urge to speak out and make suggestions about the directions that a faculty ought to take. In addition, some new faculty members will feel the urge to ask many questions to find out how some issues have reached the faculty meeting. The best advice that can be given to a new faculty member is to suppress those urges.

Most, if not all, of the topics discussed in a faculty meeting have been discussed before. There are very few new issues to reach law school faculty meetings. All of the possibilities for curriculum, class schedules, admissions, and any other faculty issue have probably already been tried. What seems like a brilliant new idea to a new faculty member was probably discussed and instituted two years ago and then discontinued one year ago because it failed. If a new faculty member spends substantial time talking about that idea in a faculty meeting, the rest of the faculty will be upset. Many new faculty members may also feel something they experienced as a student at their own law school was a good idea. No one wants to hear a new faculty member say, "When I was a (student or faculty member) at (plug in the name of any law school) we used to do it this way." It is also important to remember that no faculty wants to hear how it was done at a law firm, government office, or other law school.

Most, if not all, of the topics discussed in a faculty meeting also have a long history. This will mean that most of the faculty will have discussed the topic numerous times over many years. There will be many small facts of history that the faculty knows and accepts. Very few of the members of the faculty will enjoy restating every piece of that history for a new faculty member during the faculty meeting. Some new faculty members get to a meeting and realize that there is something about the discussion that is not clear. Those new faculty members will have an urge to begin asking questions to make sure that all facts are fully discussed in that meeting. As with the problem of raising new ideas, the best advice about asking questions is to suppress the urge.

The advice in the previous two paragraphs seems to suggest that a new faculty member should keep quiet during faculty meetings. That is, in fact, the best advice. That does not mean that a new faculty member must avoid participation in faculty governance. Just because no one wants to hear long discussions of old ideas and old facts by new faculty members, does not mean that the subject is closed. The new faculty member should make it a point to talk to senior faculty members before and after meetings. Use casual discussions outside of meetings to offer ideas and find out background facts. The senior faculty members will let the new faculty member know whether the ideas have been tried before and fill in the details of past facts. Once the new faculty member understands the background facts and knows that an idea has not been tried, then it can be offered at a faculty meeting.

A new faculty member will also be assigned to faculty committees. Work during those committees will provide substantial information about the details of the law school. The new faculty member may also have substantial opportunities to present reports and suggestions from the committee. That will give the new faculty member the chance to participate in the faculty meeting.

#### ii. Faculty Committees

All law school faculty members are assigned to law school committees. There will be standing committees dealing with issues like admission and curriculum. There will be ad hoc committees created to deal with special issues that arise on a less regular basis. A new faculty member will want to take the law school committee work seriously.

During committee meetings, senior members of the faculty will get a chance to watch a new faculty member work. A commitment to the law school, the importance of the work done, and the law school in general will be noted. A lack of commitment to those things can also be seen. Regardless of the specific committee assignment, the new faculty member must make sure that work assigned is professionally completed.

#### iii. University Service

Opportunities to provide service to the university as a whole are more difficult for a new faculty member. Senior faculty members will be servicing on The University Senate, major university committees and special university panels. Breaking into one of those major assignments takes time and some knowledge of university politics. A new faculty member probably does not want to serve on such a major university committee. Many of them are time consuming and subject to substantial internal politics.

A new faculty member should approach the law school member of the University Senate and ask for some help. That person should be able to get the new faculty member an appointment to some of the minor university committees. That will allow the new faculty member to get a feel for university politics while adding a bit of "university service" to the resume.

#### iv. Service to the Profession

Service to the profession or service to the community should be easy for the new faculty member of a law school to provide. As a lawyer, there are numerous opportunities for service to the profession and community.

The easiest way to become involved in the community is to seek out a connection to a local bar association. Most of those local bar associations have committees that are always looking for members. In addition, the new faculty member can volunteer to participate as a panelist in local bar association continuing legal education programs. Such work with a local bar association will provide the needed service while introducing the new faculty member to the local members of the profession.

A new faculty member can also begin to participate in law teaching organizations. The Association of American Law Schools, the Center for Computer Assisted Legal Instruction and SEALS are always seeking speakers, committee members and active participants. Those and other organizations provide great opportunities for service.

As a faculty member remains at a law school for a few years, opportunities for community service will expand. The chance to serve on boards, provide lectures for state wide continuing education programs, and participation as a leader in local and state bar associations will appear.

### F. Maintaining a Good Law School Presence

Through out this chapter, the topic has been how to get to tenure. It is important to make sure that the classes are taught, articles are published and service is provided. There is another issue that must be noted, but is harder to describe. A new faculty member should make an effort to be a good colleague.

If a new faculty member did all of those things mentioned throughout this chapter, there would be little time for anything else. It might seem that the new faculty member would never been seen by other faculty members because of the heavy workload. That must not happen. The new faculty member must try to be a part of the overall law school atmosphere.

The first thing the new faculty member must do is be in the law school building. It is easy to do class preparation, research, and writing from home. Much of the community service will also be done away from the law school. A faculty, however, does not want an absentee faculty member. As a first rule of work, the new faculty member should be in the building.

There are, of course, some reasons that the new faculty member must be in the building. There are classes to be taught and office hours to be maintained. It would not hurt, however, to have coffee or tea in the break room. If some of the faculty members eat lunch together, then be a part of that group. There are many advantages to be gained from some casual connections. Those casual conversations will fill in details about teaching, research and law school history that are just not available otherwise.

A new faculty member should also make it a point to be a part of law school activities. There will be speakers, alumnae events, dinners and parties. Those types of events will allow the new faculty member to meet alumnae and important community leaders. They will also provide the opportunity to further connect with faculty colleagues.

It may seem that a new faculty member should not have to dedicate a portion of his or her personal life to the law school. It could be said that the law school is merely a job for which one is paid. The more personal connection to the law school and law school colleagues, however, will be beneficial. It will be good for the career as senior colleagues get a chance to learn more about the whole person. In addition, it will make for a more interesting life and career in law teaching.

### G. Avoid the Outside Work

As should be clear from all that has been stated in this chapter, the years leading up to tenure are busy, hectic times. New classes, new research, new committees and just moving into a new city will be overwhelming. Unfortunately, the salary may not be everything that was expected when that first job was taken. Law school faculty members find numerous opportunities to earn additional money outside the law school. Local and national attorneys will call and offer consulting opportunities. The chance to arbitrate or mediate will be attractive for earning additional income. There will opportunities to teach or lecture in other schools or programs for pay. Some new faculty members may even find it possible to run a little part time law practice while teaching in law school. A new faculty member should avoid those distractions.

A new faculty member may feel some frustrations with that advice when it is noticed that some senior faculty members engage in consulting, arbitrating or other work. In the section of this book on the career after obtaining tenure, that issue will be addressed. During the years when tenure is trying to be earned, however, there is just too much at stake to take a chance on working outside of the law school.

It may be difficult to live on the salary being earned from the law school. If the law school is unable to pay a living wage, then the faculty member should seek another law school position or leave legal education. The time needed to be a good law school teacher is too demanding to work outside the law school. Any additional time that becomes available should be reinvested in teaching or research, or, when possible, devoted to family and friends.

During the early years of a law school career, the new faculty member is learning to be a faculty member. Time has to be devoted to that activity. In addition, the failure to be a competent faculty member will result in tenure being denied and the job being lost. Senior faculty members will not be sympathetic to shortcomings when it has been apparent that the untenured faculty member was spending time consulting, arbitrating, or practicing law.

For those reasons, a new faculty member should make a decision early on. If the decision is to be a law school faculty member, then full time should be devoted to that activity. If the person wants to be a practicing lawyer, then the law school should be left and the person should reenter the practice of law.

# CHAPTER 4 - LIFE AFTER TENURE

For a faculty member in the first few years of law school teaching, the tenure decision seems a long way in the future. In addition, it seems like the ultimate goal of any life. For many new faculty members it seems that tenure will never come. For most law school faculty members, however, tenure is ultimately granted. A faculty member suddenly finds him or herself with tenure and the prospects of a lifetime guaranteed job. For some, the realization that tenure has finally been reached is something of an odd feeling. There is this feeling of, "What do I do now?"

During the period before tenure, the work life is very ordered and demanding. The tenure and personal documents of the law school will dictate what the new faculty member must do. That new faculty member will feel like he or she is always struggling to complete those requirements. After tenure is granted, it may seem that there is no order or structure to the job. The tenured faculty member can do anything. The rest of this book will try to give faculty members some ideas about how to continue working in legal education and actually enjoy it.

## A. Do Not Stop Working

There are horrible jokes and stories that are told about tenured university faculty members. Those stories talk about how those teachers rarely show up for class, are never in the building, and when they do teach a class, the notes they used are yellow and brittle with age. Those same tenured faculty members are accused of having not done any research or publications since the day tenure was granted. Even if such stories are not true, there may be some faculty members that allow themselves to fall into a similar pattern. After spending six or seven years working diligently to gain tenure, there may be a feeling of being able to relax a bit. That tendency to relax may lead to a drop off of productivity. The newly tenured faculty member must fight that urge to relax. Instead, the newly tenured faculty member should look upon the changed status as a time to expand, grow and experiment with new ideas.

Some subsequent chapters will talk about lifetime teaching, lifetime research and lifetime service. All of those are possible and lead to exciting careers. There are, however, changes that can be made to move away from just those activities. This chapter will talk about some of those options.

The major point to be made, however, is that the tenured faculty member must not quite working. Students rely on serious, up to date teachers. A faculty member who does not update and revise materials is cheating the students. The amount of work to be accomplished after the grant of tenure is even larger then that before tenure. The advantage to tenure is that the type of work does not have to be dictated by the promotion and tenure document of the law school.

### B. Changing Schools

A tenured faculty member may consider changing law schools. It was a difficult job finding that first position in legal education and may seem odd that people would ever want to leave it. Many faculty members, however, move around throughout the career.

It is not necessary to wait until tenure in granted before moving to another law school. For a faculty member seeking a permanent move, it may even be easier to make that move before tenure is granted. Before tenure, the salary is lower, and a new school may not feel the financial pinch to offer higher money. There are even opportunities to visit at other law schools before tenure. Many law schools like to fill in vacancies for one semester or one year with someone who will not demand a high salary.

Whether the thought about changing schools occurs before or after tenure, it is a thought that should be addressed. There are generally two types of moves. A faculty member may seek to visit another school for one semester or one year. A visiting faculty member will usually be asked to teach a course load that is temporarily open because of a vacancy. A permanent move is one where the faculty member actually becomes part of the faculty of the new school. After the brief discussion of moving to other law schools in this chapter, there is a more detailed discussion of transferring in chapter 8.

i. Visiting

There are several positive advantages to be gained by visiting at another law school. It gives the faculty member a chance to see what other law schools are like. It broadens one's view of legal education. It may also provide an incentive to move permanently to another law school. For the faculty member that is feeling some post tenure decision let down, it may also be a way to add sufficient change in one's life to perk up the career.

Visiting positions actually may come in two different types. There are the "real" visiting positions. Those are positions where a law school has a short term opening and wants someone to fill it for a short period of time. The opening may be due to a regular faculty member being away for a year or it may be a special distinguished visiting position to bring in special visitors. Those "real" visiting positions will be for a term of one semester or one year. Some law schools use the position of a visitor for a "look-see" with the possibility of hiring the visitor for a full time position in the future. The "look-see" visit gives a law school an opportunity to have a faculty member around the school for a lengthy period of time to determine whether there is a good fit for a permanent hire. Either way, the visiting position gives the faculty member a chance to do something different for awhile. It may also lead to a permanent move.

There are probably two ways to seek a visiting position. The first is to use the Association of American Law Schools (AALS) "Visiting Faculty Register." The web site for the AALS can provide detailed information about this service together with the necessary form. The information is provided to law schools in October and February of each year.

The second method of obtaining a visiting position is through connections. Visiting positions are usually offered to fill a specific teaching slot. Schools need someone to teach in a particular area and want a good teacher. A person looking for a visiting position may want to call colleagues and friends around the county to find out if visiting slots are available. It is also advisable to attend conference, give talks and be a productive scholar if there is some thought that visiting might be something desirable in the future. Having one's name known in legal education is a good way to attract visiting opportunities.

ii. Permanent Move

A faculty member may decide that he or she wants to go to another law school on a permanent basis. As with getting the first position, it is possible to use the AALS placement conference to seek a full time position. Many of the positions offered through the placement conference, however, are entry level positions. It is more likely that finding a position for a permanent move may require using contacts made at conferences, through publications or other routes.

It should be noted that many permanent moves arise after having completed a visiting position at an institution. As noted above, many law schools use visiting positions as a "look-see" for making hires of faculty members above the entry level. If a law school wants to hire a tenured faculty member, that law school will probably invite the person for a one years visit first. If the visit goes well, a permanent position may be offered. Usually the terms and conditions of such a "look-see" are discussed before the visit begins.

A faculty member will know whether a visit is a "true visit" or actually a "look-see" for a permanent position.

There is also the possibility of looking for a move to take a "distinguished chair." Most universities provide additional funding for such positions. The extra funding may come from donors or from the university's own funds. The position will usually carry the name of the primary donor.

A distinguished chair usually arises when a major donor decides that he or she wants the law school to have a specialist in some particular area. That donor will provide sufficient money to set up an endowment to fund that chair. The endowment may provide funds for a salary, travel, secretarial help and other benefits. The holder of the chair will be expected to teach and write in the designated area.

Since the distinguished chairs carry such benefits, law schools usually conduct a nationwide search for a known expert. The school will usually be looking for someone with a known record of teaching and publications in the specific area. In order to be seriously considered for such positions, it will be necessary for the faculty member to have such a resume. The distinguished chair may require a certain subject area and will definitely require extensive experience. Before considering applying for such a chair, a faculty member should realistically think about his or her resume. If it does not have the full range of materials that will meet the requirements of the chair, the position should not be sought.

In seeking to fill such positions, law schools usually advertise widely. They will run ads in the ABA journal, the Chronicle of Higher Education, and then send letters to all of the law schools. If a faculty member is interested in applying for such positions, it is only necessary to check those sources. There are usually a few of those positions being advertised each year.

### C. Do You Want to be a Dean?

There comes a time in every law school faculty member's career when he or she begins to wonder if being a dean would be a good idea. Deans do not have special training or skills and, for the most part, come from the ranks of tenured faculty members. For any tenured faculty member, the possibility of becoming a dean may be considered.

Before even considering the possibility of becoming a dean, a faculty member should note one initial issue. Most law schools do a national search and select a dean from outside the law school faculty. The issue of whether that is a good or bad idea is outside the scope of this text. The reason it is mentioned is to alert faculty members to that fact. If a faculty member wants to be a dean of a law school that will probably require a move to a different law school. A faculty member who has been involved in legal education long enough to consider being a dean may look at his or her own institution to see the reality of that fact. If the university administration has hired the last 4 or 5 deans from the outside, it is unlikely that a sudden change in practice will occur. Such a faculty member may assume that all future deans will also be hired from the outside.

If a faculty member believes that he or she would like to be a dean, the road to a deanship should be reviewed. Most deans have some administrative experience. This means that most deans have been an associate dean before becoming a dean. If, therefore, a faculty member believes that he or she may want to be a dean, seek out an appointment as an associate dean. First, most law schools change associates deans on a regular basis. The new associate deans are usually taken from the full time faculty at that law school. For someone thinking about being a dean, getting a position as an associate dean should not be difficult.

There are several things about the associate dean experience that are helpful. Gaining the practical knowledge as an associate dean is something that most law schools expect to see in hiring a dean. In that regard, it fills the resume with the needed items. More importantly, it gives the faculty member a taste of law school administration. There are many faculty members who thought they might like to be a dean until they spent a few years as an associate dean. After that experience, they decided that being a dean was not for them. Anyone thinking about being a dean should, therefore, spend a few years as an associate dean.

If someone wants to be a dean, he or she should talk to a dean. It may appear that a dean is an academic scholar who provides the educational leadership to the law school. That may be a part of the job, but there are many more tasks associated with the position. Universities and law schools are big business. Budgets at law schools run into the millions of dollars. A dean must be something of a financial manager in order to control and use such a budget. Law schools also have a large number of employees. When the numbers of faculty members, librarians, secretaries, and other support staff are added together, the size of the employment pool at a law school is larger then many businesses. A dean must be a good employee relations manager. Most law schools are part of a larger university. Those universities are run by boards through a president and vice-presidents. There are deans of other units that will be fighting to get the attention of and funding from the president. The law school dean must be able to be a strong advocate for the law school in the highly competitive bureaucracy. Higher education is notoriously under-funded in the United States. One of the only sources for additional funding is from members of the community and alumnae. The dean must be an outstanding fund raiser.

In addition to all of those talents, a dean must be a good public speaker. Because of the very public nature of the position of Dean, the person who holds that office must present a good public persona. The Dean will be making speeches before large audiences of students, alumnae groups, legislators and judges. The Dean will also be talking to small groups at legislative hearings, alumnae committee meetings, and university meetings. In addition, the Dean will have to be able to chat with people at parties, receptions and social gatherings. Most people are aware of whether they are able to make the kind of public presentations in those wide ranging circumstances. If a person is not able to operate in all of those areas, that person should not seek the position of Dean.

If a faculty member decides that he or she still wants to be a dean after considering all of those facts, that faculty member should begin to look for advertisements for deanships. It is speculated that approximately 1/3 of the law schools in the United States are looking for a new dean each year. The opportunities for finding a deanship are there. Schools seeking a dean usually advertise in the ABA journal, the Chronicle of Higher Education and then send letters to all other law schools.

### D. Consulting and Outside Work

In the chapter on "Getting to Tenure," it was suggested that the new faculty member avoid consulting or work outside the law school. The risks were considered too high for the amount of money likely to be gained. Once tenure has been obtained, the factors concerning outside work change. There may be opportunities for such work.

A faculty member who decides to begin consulting or doing some outside work should remember to remain committed to legal education. It is very easy for a faculty member to begin with a small bit of consulting and wind up spending more time practicing law then teaching. Tax work, labor arbitrations and mediations, and brief writing can consume huge amounts of time. The financial rewards may seem great, but the loss of commitment to the law school will be serious.

There are, of course, areas of consulting and outside work that are financially helpful and helpful to the law school career. Names of well known faculty members taking a leave from a law school to be a special prosecutor are easily found. Some well known faculty members find it possible to regular move between the law school setting and government service. Those types of work provide exciting outlets for the faculty member and name recognition for the law school.

Some faculty members may occasionally consult on major cases. It is possible to limit time in consulting and be a major part of landmark litigation. That type of work is also generally helpful to both the faculty member and law school.

Although unpaid, some faculty members use free time to engage in pro bono work. That work may be done for national groups, local agencies, or on small one to one opportunities. If the work is done as a part of community service it is also a welcome addition to the career.

The type of work to be avoided is that which becomes a second career while the faculty member is supposed to be a full time member of the faculty. Such work becomes the primary focus of the faculty member and the law school work suffers.

### E. Be a Mentor

Through the chapter on "Getting to Tenure," it was advised that a new faculty member should frequently seek the advice of a mentor. After getting to tenure, a faculty member should make it a point to be a mentor. After six to eight years of hard work, the faculty member will suddenly realize that there are now other new faculty members who are trying to figure out how to survive in the law school setting. Each faculty member has a duty to help those new faculty members survive and thrive in the law school. It is actually to the law schools advantage to have new faculty members be successful. Having a bright energetic group of new teachers and researchers will help the law school continue to grow and improve. This can only be done with the help and guidance of the newest member of the "senior faculty."

Being a mentor is not that difficult. It can begin by being available to newer faculty member. A tenured faculty member should stop into a new faculty member's office and offer to help. That offer may be to assist in setting in on a class, giving teaching advice, discussing the tenure requirements, reading over first drafts of research or just being available to discuss the nature of the law teaching job. Keep in mind that not everyone will want to accept the offers of help. Mentoring cannot be forced on anyone. When a new faculty member does not seem interested in accepting the offered help, the tenured faculty member should remain patient. The new faculty member may be getting help from someone else or may just not need the assistance.

# CHAPTER 5 - LIFETIME RESEARCH AND WRITING

One of the ways of enjoying the rest of the career after tenure is to continue a lifetime of research and writing. There are, of course, stories of tenured faculty members that never publish another piece after tenure. Such behavior hurts the law school and denies the students the most up to date information and ideas. It also denies the faculty member the opportunity for continued advancement, distinguished chairs, raises, invitations to speak and other benefits that should come with being a law school faculty member.

Most importantly, it denies the faculty member the enjoyment of a lifetime of learning. People should go into university teaching because they enjoy learning and sharing what they have learned with others. It is not possible for a university faculty member to continue to learn unless he or she continues to research and write. The post-tenure years are a great time to study all of those issues for which there was no time to study in the past. For those that enjoying studying, researching, learning and writing, the post-tenure years are the most enjoyable years of the career. For those who do not enjoy such activities, they should not be in the law school teaching. They have chosen a career for which they cannot enjoy a major portion of the job. Continuing with research, writing and publication is an excellent way to occupy one's mine with the great possibilities in the law. This chapter will offer some advice on how to make research, writing and publications a regular part of a faculty member's extended career.

## A. Continue the Work You Started

The easiest way to continue research is to continue the research conducted while trying to get tenure. No area of the law is stagnant. Every area of the law continues to grow and change. New cases, statutes and regulations appear every day that create changes in the law. New research, suggestions and ideas appear in law journals that seek to reinterpret the law that exists. A tenured faculty member can be a part of the dialog. The article that a new faculty member wrote during the first year of law teaching is now probably out of date and was not that great when it was written. Many law teachers find that on rereading an old article they are shocked at how they would change it if they were to write it today. An experienced researcher and law teacher can rethink that old material. That old article can be updated and expanded to include new ideas.

In teaching and researching, most areas continue to suggest new and related topics. Courses like torts, contracts, property, securities regulations, corporations, and most others have more issues then any one faculty member could research in a lifetime. Questions asked in class by students can spark a thought about a new article. It should be impossible for any law teacher to ever reach a point where they feel that every issue in their area of expertise has been completely researched. If earlier articles were written in the area of one's teaching assignments, surely those courses suggest other issues that can be researched.

If the tenured faculty member still has difficulty finding topics, then that faculty member should look back at that little notebook that was suggested for the untenured faculty member. In an earlier chapter of this book, it was suggested that an untenured faculty member keep a small notebook of ideas. Those ideas could be researched when the time was available. The tenure faculty member should go back through that notebook and pick out topics.

### B. Begin to Research New Areas

It is possible, of course, that after the seven year period of seeking tenure, the faculty member has just grown weary of researching the same topics. The post tenure period is an excellent time to begin looking into new topics. Although a tenured faculty member needs to continue to be productive, the pressure is over to produce articles within specific time periods and have them published in specific journals. A tenured faculty member can begin to look at new areas without fear of taking longer or running into dead ends. The post tenure time is the perfect opportunity to begin to research and learn about a topic that has always been of some interest but too difficult to pursue.

### C. Look Into Formats other than Journal Articles

It was suggested that during the tenure period the new faculty member should probably adhere to writing traditional law review articles. The law review format is the safest form of publication to ensure a smooth path to tenure. After tenure, the faculty member can begin to experiment with other formats. There is almost an infinite variety of publication types that are available. As with new topics, new formats can allow the faculty member to experiment. The pressure to publish within a particular time frame is no longer a concern. In addition, the advice to avoid co-authorship is also relaxed after tenure. Making contacts and putting together projects with colleagues from around the country can be an interesting and worthwhile activity after tenure.

Moving from the traditional law review to shorter articles for bar association publications is an easy transition. Most bar association publications are constantly seeking articles. The editors of the magazines enjoy working with law teachers for several reasons. Law teachers usually bring a level of expertise and insight that is different from the practitioner. The law faculty member is use to writing articles and will submit the article on time and in good shape. That is not always true of practitioners who write articles.

When writing for bar association publications, however, it is necessary to make the articles applicable to the practitioner and judges. That will require the law professor to add more of a practical slant to the article then those written for law reviews. This necessity, however, is good for the law professor. This allows the faculty member to begin to think about the legal issues with a practical application. Once such articles are written, the faculty member will find that carrying that information back to the classroom will make the class more interesting for the students.

Most newspapers seek articles, letters, or columns concerning legal issues. If the local editor finds a law faculty member willing to write on a broad range of subjects, then the faculty member will find him or herself frequently asked to contribute.

Moving from articles to books is also a natural progression. After having written several articles on a topic, bringing all of the information together in a book is a reasonable expectation. After having taught a course for some years, working on a book within that topic can also be a reasonable project.

Finding the book topic should be easy for a faculty member that has been in teaching for over seven years. There would be those topics that were researched during the tenure process that could be expanded to book length. There would be those gaps in theoretical material that were noticed when doing the research on those early articles. For the experienced teacher, there will be noticed gaps in class materials that offer the opportunity for book writing. For the faculty member that has spent substantial time preparing his or her own teaching materials, the possibility of having those materials published in book form should be exciting. Some faculty members are able to take the theoretical material and turn it into practical material for lawyers and judges. Book publishers are always looking for books to sell to practitioners. For the faculty member that can write such books, that is a good opportunity for book writing.

Preparing the first book is also an excellent time to begin working with co-authors. Writing a book takes a substantial amount of time. For many first time book authors, it comes as a real surprise as to how difficult the task of book writing really is. Compiling the information, organizing it into a book length project and then taking the time necessary to produce a project that long is substantially greater then creating a law review article. For those reasons, working with co-authors and dividing the chapters among several people makes it easier for the first project. Having a few co-authors also helps sales of the book. The more authors on the cover the greater the likelihood that those authors will be encouraging people to read the book.

The idea of book sales is one of the additional benefits of book writing. Unlike law review articles, book publishers pay the authors of books for doing the work. This is actually a type of work outside the law school that is favored by most law schools. The law school gets to claim a book author on the faculty while the faculty member is earning a little extra money. For the tenured faculty member, the prospect of book writing, gaining additional appreciation from the law school, gaining recognition in the law teaching profession and making addition money is an attractive combination. Getting the book contract, however, is not as easy as finding a place to get a law review article published.

## D. Getting that Book Contract

### i. Writing that Book is Harder Then it Looks

Before a faculty member decides to try to get a book contract, there should be some warning about the difficulties that lie ahead. Writing a book is a difficult undertaking. The time and effort that is needed to complete the project will come as a surprise to a first time book writer.

For a faculty members who wrote a graduate degree thesis or faculty members who have written longer law review articles, some idea of the nature of the task can be seen. Finishing a book, however, is many times harder then finishing the thesis or law review article.

The difficulty in finishing a book will come as a surprise to many who have never written one. They will notice some prolific writers who seem to turn out one or more books a year. It will seem that if such projects are so easy for some, surely writing one book cannot be that difficult.

It was noted in the sections on research and writing, that writing is an activity that is done alone. Book writing stretches that period of working alone. For those who find it difficult to work alone, finishing a book will be impossible.

It is obvious that a book is much longer then a graduate thesis or an article. The length by itself adds problems. The writer must be able to organize a larger amount of material and keep it organized throughout the whole text. In addition, the writer will need to be able remain focused on the whole text throughout the period necessary to complete it.

For the faculty member who is able to write a book, write it well and finish it on time, the door to future books will open immediately. Publishers are always looking for people who can complete the task. For the faculty member who gets a book contract and is unable to finish it, that will probably be the last book contract that he or see will see.

Because of the difficulty in finishing a book, this may be a good time to work with a co-author. Agreeing to write a couple of chapters in a book is a good way to find out about the efforts necessary to writing a book. It will give the new book author a chance to find out what is necessary and decide if the additional effort to complete an entire book is even possible.

#### ii. Getting the Book Contract is Difficult

When a faculty member writes a law review article there is some general expectation that it can be published somewhere. There are approximately 200 accredited law schools in the United States and they all have at least one law review. Some of those law schools have multiple law reviews. There are numerous bar association publications, ABA publications, and other similar law journals. In addition, there are numerous law reviews and magazines published outside the United States for those who write in selected areas. Finding a place to publish a law review article is not difficult. The same cannot be said for law books.

The publishing industry, like many other industries, has gone through substantial changes over the past 40 years. Once there were many law book publishers. These publishers were small to medium companies that published a range of books in a variety of specialties. An author seeking a publisher could contact dozens of publishers with ideas. Over the years, the number of law book publishers continued to shrink as companies merged or were bought up by a few multi-national organizations. Those large companies could cut costs and ultimately drove smaller companies out of business. Having just a few large companies reduced the options for a new author looking for a publisher. Those companies could control the market and were interested in publishing books that sold to the widest audience.

Over the past 5 to 10 years, however, a new trend has emerged. Using modern technology, small publishing companies have begun to open, seek a niche, and grow into successful operations. The trend has made it possible for new authors to have again a wider range of publishers with which to work. It should be possible within the next few years for many new authors to find a publishing house for new works. Finding that first book publishing contract, however, is still hard.

Book publishers are more likely to offer a contract to an author that has already published a few books. The reason for this should be obvious. That author already has a track record. The publishing company can rely on the author getting the work in on time an in the proper format. The author understands book publishing and will not be difficult to work with. In addition, the author already has an audience. The book publisher can rely on some immediate sales to those who are familiar with the author's work.

The tendency to offer contracts to those who have already published books makes it difficult for the first time author to get the first contract. It will take some effort to get that first contract. If, however, the author does a good job with the first contract, prepares the material well and on time, then future contracts are much easier to obtain.

In seeking that first book contract, it is advantageous to find faculty members who already have book contracts. A faculty member can talk to members of his or her own faculty and determine who is a book writer. If there are some on the faculty, seek their help. They should be able to offer advice on publishers, topics, and areas of interest of those publishers. If there are no book writers on one's own faculty the prospective book writer should begin to look for people around the country. It is possible that law teachers met at conferences or visits to other schools will be able to offer advice and guidance. One of the real advantages of seeking advice from current book writers is that such people may be looking for a co-author. If a colleague hears of one's interest and offers a chance to co-author something already under contract, that is the best opportunity to get that first book contract.

If no book writing colleagues can be found, talk to publishers at the annual AALS conference. During that annual conference, there is a large room set up for companies to offer goods and services to law teachers. All book publishing companies that supply law books will attend that conference. The publishing companies that attend may also be willing to begin preliminary discussions about possible book titles. Talk to someone in each booth and get the name of the appropriate person for discussing book ideas. If that person is attending the conference, make an appointment to talk to that person while at the conference. If that person is not at the conference, get his or her address and contact them later. For large companies, there may be different people in charge of different areas of the law. A new prospective author needs to make sure that he or she has the right contact person for the project. A substantial amount of time can be wasted by talking to someone that has no authority to make a decision on a particular topic.

There is an interesting point about the companies attending the AALS conference. For the large publishing companies, they tend to divide the company between law school books and law practice books. The people attending the AALS conference will be working for that portion of the company that deals with law school books. If the faculty member has an idea for a book that will be marketed to law students, it will be easy to find someone to talk to at the AALS conference.

For the faculty member seeking to publish law practice books, it will be hard to get information about that part of the company. The publishing companies do not tend to send representatives to the AALS conference who work in the area of the company that markets books to the practicing bar. Information about contacts for law practice books will have to be gained by contacting the company directly, seeking information on the company's web site, or attending the annual ABA convention and talking with the publishing companies there.

Once the appropriate person within the publishing company has been identified, it is time to send a proposal. It is better to have had some initial contact with that person to make sure they are expecting the proposal. Mailing in a large packet of information to someone not expecting it will probably result in it not being reviewed.

The initial proposal should have several distinct parts. First, it is necessary to write a short description of what the book will be about. This description should talk about the nature of the book, the appropriate audience, and the general themes that will be addressed. It will be helpful to the publisher to explain what other books are currently available in that general area and how the new book will fill a specific need. The description should also give some estimate of the number of pages in the final text and when the final draft could be ready. Second, the proposal packet should contain an outline of the entire text. That outline should be sufficiently detailed in order to allow the publisher to determine exactly what will be covered in the book. Third, the proposal packet should contain a resume of the author. Hopefully, this resume can highlight the prior writings and publications of the proposing author. This will allow the publisher to determine whether the author will be able to complete the proposed project.

The publisher will want to take some time to review the proposal. That review may likely involve several different reviewers. The person with the decision making authority will want the proposal reviewed by editors in the company that will work with the book. The company may, in fact, have an outside editorial board of lawyers, judges and law professors who will have to review the proposal. Depending on the company, the review may take a few days to several months. It is appropriate to ask how long the review process should take. In waiting for a response, it would not be appropriate to be submitting the book to other publishing companies. Most companies will have to expend some time and money in conducting the review. There is an expectation that the author will wait for an answer before sending the book to other publishers.

Many first time book writers will already have a fairly complete idea of what they want the book to look like. For those who want to publish class room teaching materials, they may already have it prepared. For those who want to write a book of text for classes or materials for practitioners, they may be ready to begin the actual writing. The question may arise as to whether the new author should write the book before it is accepted or wait for a contract. If the book is already written, it can be sent with the letter of proposal. If the book is not written, the new author may want to wait for a contract before completing the work. Nothing could be more frustrating then having a book length manuscript sitting on a shelf and never published.

There are, of course, alternatives to either writing the full book or waiting for a contract. For materials to be used in classes, nothing should stop the faculty member from preparing the material and using it in his or her own classes. The materials may never be published, but they will be used throughout a career. For other texts, there is a more difficult issue. One solution is to write the text in clear, distinct chapters. Those chapters can be written so that they can be divided into individual law review articles. If the new author is unable to get a book publishing contact, the chapters can be divided and published as a series of articles.

Once the contract is offered, there are a series of questions that the author will have to address. There may be some tendency to feel that substantial time must be spent reviewing and negotiating the contract. That probably will not happen. Most publishing companies have developed a standard contract and that is the one they will offer. If the author does not like the contract, it can be refused. It will probably not be re-negotiated.

Payment for the work may be made in one of two ways. Most publishing companies will offer royalties based on sales of the books. The royalties may range from 10% to 20% with around 15% being the most common. It would be rare for a publishing company to offer an advance on that royalty. In addition, the company will usually supply the author between 5 to 10 copies of the finished work. Royalties will probably be paid every six months. The contract will usually give the author the right of first refusal on writing updates and supplements to the book.

A few publishing companies may have a different way of compensating an author. Such publishing companies may offer a one time payment for the writing of a book. Under those terms, the publishing company will pay the author for the work when the manuscript is submitted. The submission and payment ends the relationship between the company and the author. Such a contract will usually not offer complimentary copies nor the right to prepare supplements.

A new author should keep in mind that very few law book authors make substantial money. The royalties may rise, fall or stop completely. A new author should not ever feel dependent on book royalties. For the book writer, however, the royalties together with royalties on all future supplements makes a nice little addition to one's income.

iii. Writing the Book

It was noted earlier that getting the book contract and actually writing the book is hard. A few words of advice on how to get the book written should be given. The primary thing to remember is that the due date will actually show up in the future. The contract will provide a specific date that the manuscript is to be submitted. That date may be as much as a year in the future. It will seem to some that a year is plenty of time to research and write a book. It is easy to put off work on a project that is not due for a year. It will not be possible to write a book in a short period of time just before the due date, so the work must be begun immediately.

The author should already have a good outline of the book that was submitted in seeking the contract. That outline is a good place to start. The author should carefully go over the outline and make sure it is still appropriate. Any changes, additions or deletions should be made. The author should then use the outline to mark up shorter due dates for each section. These intermediate due dates should allow the author to be finished with the first draft of the manuscript about two months before the book is due at the publisher. Those final two months can then be used to finish anything that is left over while doing proof reading, editing and re-writing. A good example might be a book contract that is due one year in the future and will have 10 chapters. The author could work to finish one chapter a month while leaving the last two months for proof reading and editing.

After setting up this series of intermediate personal due dates, the author must get started. As suggested in the section on general writing, the author should set aside time on a daily basis to work on the book. It is only by consistent, daily work that the project can be finished.

If the author follows a good organized method of finishing the book, several positive things will occur. First, the book will be a better product. The time, effort and focus that were devoted to the book will allow the author to do a good job. Secondly, the publishing company will be pleased. Publishing companies consistently have authors who send in manuscripts late. When they find an author that will produce a good manuscript in a timely manner, the publishing company will be likely to offer another book contract.

### E. Podcasts, Blogs, and on the Internet

Once the pressure to write law reviews is removed, there are numerous new technologies that can be used to continuing creative activities. There is a continuing debate about the academic significance of these items and, for that reason, would not be a good choice by someone trying to get tenure. For the tenured faculty member, however, they provide new ways to experiment with research.

Blogs are the most common new technology that has found use by many people. A blog is merely an online record of what someone wants to say. Most law schools currently provide the technology to allow faculty members to start and maintain a blog. For those that do not have access to a blog through their law school, the Center for Computer Assisted Legal Instruction (CALI) provides that service on its web site.

A faculty member can start a blog to discuss areas of research or other interest. If the blog begins to attract readers, it will allow the faculty member to exchange ideas with a wide range of scholars. Even if other faculty members chose not to participate, the blogger can encourage his or her students to read and comment on the ideas. The blog allows the faculty member to hold a conversation with the world.

Another new technology is the podcast. The podcast is merely an audio recording that is stored on the internet. A faculty member can record lectures, research ideas or other discussions. The podcast can be saved to the internet at the law school, through the course management systems or at the CALI web site. As with the blog, others may be encourage to listen and make comments.

For the faculty member that wants to create an internet presence, he or she may create a web site. Working with the law school technology people should make that idea a possibility. The faculty member could then list previous publications, ideas for future publications, link to the blog, link to the podcasts, and generally open up the site for a broad discussion of interesting ideas.

In short, the use of modern technology will allow the tenured faculty member to experiment with research, writing, and creative activity in ways never dreamed years ago. This will allow the faculty member to continue to be excited by research and publications long after the tenure decision has been made

# CHAPTER 6 - LIFETIME TEACHING

Law professors are usually required to teach two courses a semester. After tenure is granted, a faculty member will continue to teach for the rest of the law teaching career. For the faculty member who enjoys teaching, the teaching will remain a fresh, exciting activity throughout that career. For even the most dedicated teacher, however, there may be times that the routine of teaching begins to get a little old. There are some techniques to help avoid that boredom. The lifelong law teacher wants to avoid the situation of teaching the same classes from the same notes for numerous years. That will not only tend to bore the faculty member, the students will find the presentation somewhat routine. The students will obtain class notes from previous students and find that the course never changes. A faculty member needs to continually renew the courses.

## A. Make Yourself an Expert in a Field

The first and most obvious solution to avoiding boredom in the classroom is for the law teacher to make him or herself an expert in the field. If the faculty member has been teaching the same course during the pre-tenure period, that faculty member will have a firm understanding of the basics. The post tenure period is the time to mix the teaching and research interest. The faculty member can begin to write articles and books on the same topic as the course topics. The preparation of publications will also begin to attract invitations for presentations. Those invitations may be from local bar associations, state bar associations or national organizations.

While increasing the connection between classes and research, the faculty member may want to create a small seminar in some specialty area of that course work. This will further allow the faculty member to be an expert in the field. That faculty member might, for example, teach the major course in Evidence, create a seminar on "Use of Expert testimony and Scientific Evidence," and then work with a law schools mock trial team. A faculty member who teaches Torts may also teach smaller courses in Products Liability and Medical Malpractice. Such a combination will deliver a valuable package to the school and students while keeping the excitement in classroom teaching. The creation of small specialty seminars is an activity that can continue throughout a faculty member's career. Although Evidence and Torts were used as the example, every area of law can be expanded in the same way.

Every area of the law is broad and subject to continuing growth. The advantage to working on being an expert in a particular field is that it allows the faculty member to continue to be excited about that field. A topic that is ripe for a seminar or a major research project today may fade from importance several years from now. At that point, the faculty member could pick another topic within the major field to use for research and a seminar. The point of being an expert in the field is the ability to constantly stay interested in the changing issues that are a part of that field.

### B. Constantly Change Your Classes

#### i. Update your notes

There may be a tendency among some faculty members to become a bit complacent with the classes. After having taught the same class for seven years during the pre-tenure period, there may be a feeling that all is known about that subject. It would be easy to continue to use the same notes for each succeeding year. The only mandatory time to change the class would occur when the editors of the case book that is used decide to bring out a new edition. A faculty member should work to avoid becoming that complacent.

A faculty member who teaches the same classes each year should work to update the class notes every year. It would not be necessary to completely change the presentation each year, but changing portions of the material is necessary.

In each class, there are some days that the class goes well and some that it does not. The faculty member should make notes about those facts and change the material that is not working. In addition, the faculty member should constantly read current material in his or her area. That reading should include new law review articles, cases, statutes, regulations and other sources. After reading such material, the new ideas should be incorporated into the class notes.

For the faculty member who is actively engaged in research, publications and presentation, finding new material for the class is easy. The research for publications and the questions asked during outside presentations will provide new material for law school classes.

A faculty member who frequently changes and updates the class notes will accomplish many positive things. The students will enjoy the classes and be pleased with the obvious fresh approach taken each year. The faculty member will be able to remain interested and fresh in teaching the same class each year.

ii. Change books

Some faculty members feel it is necessary to change the primary text that is used for the class on a regular basis. This allows the faculty member to completely renew the class notes and presentation. A different casebook, for example, will have different cases, different organization, and a different underlying approach to the material. By changing the basic text, the faculty member will find the new challenge a good way to renew his or her own interest in the material.

Even if a faculty member decides not to adopt a different primary text, that faculty member should regularly review different books. By reviewing those different books, the faculty member is able to see the different cases and the different approaches. That faculty member can then use some of that different material to update and refresh his or her own class.

iii. Prepare your own teaching materials

At some point in a law teacher's career, that faculty member should begin to prepare his or her own class materials. After teaching the same area for several years, the faculty member will become familiar with cases, statutes or whole areas that can be expanded. That faculty member can begin to put together a packet of class materials for the students to use as a supplement to the course. Those additional materials may include cases, statutes, regulations, problems, law review articles, or anything else that the faculty member wants to include.

With the explosion of new technology, the faculty member can remain excited about a course and continue to update it by working with some of that new technology. There are several items in the new technology that can be used easily from the very beginning. With further use, the faculty member can experiment with the more complex features of the items.

The first step should be to use and expand an online course management system. As mentioned in other sections, there are at least three different providers of on line course management systems. Blackboard is a system generally offered and used by most universities. In addition, both West and Lexis have their own systems. It is possible to begin easily by posting a syllabus, class schedule and basic course information on the site. Over time, the faculty member can add problems, quizzes, special materials and other features.

Second, the faculty member could begin to use a few basic power point slides to enhance certain parts of the class. Power point is, of course, a well known and frequently used type of software. It is possible to make slides showing items that a whole class needs to see. Posting statutes, regulations, case quotations, problems or future assignments can be easily done. It is possible to prepare these before class and have them readily available at the appropriate time.

The faculty member could then begin to use podcasts, a blog, CALI lessons and any number of additional features. Once the faculty member begins to use some of the modern technology, there are a wide range of items that can be found. The addition of all of those items can begin very simply and allowed to grow.

The students will be very comfortable with the use of technology because they are already using most of it in their daily life. Students can access on line course management systems to check assignments and other postings. Students can check the blogs in order to be a part of an on line discussion. Students can also download pod casts to a MP3 player to listen to in the future. The faculty member will find it exciting to see how technology can be used to create a positive atmosphere for learning among the students.

**C. Finding a New Area**

If all of the above fails to keep the tenured faculty member interested in the classes, there is another alternative. The faculty member can decide to move into another area for teaching. With the natural turnover that occurs in law school faculties, openings will occur in different subject areas. A faculty member who is getting bored with a subject area should watch for such an opening. When the law school is noting that a subject area is starting to need new people, a tenured faculty member can volunteer to step into that area.

Some faculty members may find that some of the changes seem like a natural progression. A faculty member who teaches "Gift and Estate Tax" may offer to teach "Wills and Trusts." A faculty member who teaches "Evidence" may offer to teach "Trial Practice." A faculty member who has taught such courses as

"Torts," "Contracts," or "Civil Procedure" may offer to teach "Legal History."

Other changes may not be obvious to colleagues, but will be attractive to the faculty member making the change. A faculty member who majored in "Philosophy" in undergraduate or graduate school may offer to teach "Jurisprudence." A faculty member who majored in "History" in undergraduate or graduate school may offer to teach "Legal History."

There could still be other changes that would not be obvious to anyone. A faculty member could have always had an interest in a topic and wanted to know more about it. Offering to teach a course in a personal topic of interest will ensure that much is learned about that topic.

Considering picking up a new course in a new area is something that every tenured faculty member should do during his or her career. It will provide a great benefit to the law school. That topic would have gone untaught, or required the hiring of a new faculty member or adjunct to get it into the curriculum. Having a tenured faculty member pick up the course simplifies the issue. Picking up a new course may also provide the type of rejuvenation that a tenure faculty member periodically needs. The excitement and challenge of that new course will improve the overall work atmosphere for that faculty member.

# CHAPTER 7 - LIFETIME SERVICE

A service commitment is expected of all law school faculty members. During the pre-tenure years that is usually seen as serving on law school committees and trying to work into some community service. The post tenure years offer expanded opportunities for service. By the time tenure is granted, the faculty member may have been in the same law school, university and community for over seven years. There has been sufficient time to get to know people and issues facing all of those. A faculty member who remains content to attend faculty meetings and serve on a few law school committees is missing a great opportunity. Expanding one's service is a way to provide needed help to many people while making one's work more interesting. In addition, for those law faculty members who wish to become Deans of a law school or move into university administration, gaining further experience in a variety of university and law school committee work is almost necessary.

## A. Moving up in University Faculty Governance

Some faculty members find working in University Governance to be an exciting opportunity. Most universities have some type of representative faculty senate. Law school faculty members are usually attractive to those organizations due to the legal background. A law faculty member that wants to be a part of the University governance can start by being the law school representative to that group. By remaining in that group, that faculty member can become active in major university committees and may, ultimately, be president or chairman of the organization.

In addition to the university senates, there are other types of university committee work that can be interesting. Universities must undergo accreditation reviews approximately every 10 years. The work necessary to prepare preliminary reports is broad and time consuming. Numerous members of the university faculty must participate to prepare those materials. For law faculty members interested in the broader university may find that such work is exciting.

Universities have athletic programs that have become big business. Most universities will have faculty committees that review and oversee some aspects of the athletic program. Many faculty members find that such committee work fulfills the service requirement while meeting their interest in sports.

Once a faculty member has been at a university long enough to receive tenure, that faculty member will have learned that the number of university committees seems, at times, infinite. For almost any interest within the university setting, there is a committee to discuss and oversee it. A faculty member who is looking for university wide activities, a little work in seeking out such committees is all that is necessary to become involved.

### B. Committee Work in the Law School

All law school faculty members will be assigned to work on law school committees. Some, if not most, faculty members may see this as a necessary, but unattractive, part of the job. In order to enhance the enjoyment of the position, a faculty member may try to position him or herself in committee assignments that are more enjoyable.

For some faculty members, volunteering for important committee assignments is a way to be a part of issues in the law school. Committees to hire new faculty members or a new dean may have an impact on the law school for years to come. Such committees are hard work, but can be rewarding when good decisions are made. Committees that admit students will have a direct impact on the nature of the student body. Being a part of that committee will allow the faculty member to have a dramatic impact on life within the law school.

Since law school committees are a fact of a law teacher's life, a faculty member should try to get the most out of those committees as possible. Seek to find committees that are interesting and challenging. The committee work in a law school will be time consuming so the faculty member should try to make sure it adds to the enjoyment of the job.

### C. Provide Service to the Profession

Service to the profession and the community may provide the best opportunity to gaining a variety of experiences while being a law teacher. It is expected, for example, that all law faculty members will provide some connection to bar associations and the AALS. Basic attendance at meetings and participation in some events will be routine. A law faculty member should seek to expand beyond that basic expectation.

The easiest way to engage in further service to the profession is to become an active participant in local and state bar associations. Those organizations have administrative committees, continuing education programs, law reform groups, and publications. They usually have more work to be done then volunteers willing to do it. Once the class schedule is set, a law faculty member is usually able to make sure that he or she attends all meetings, completes any work assignment and does those things on time. A practicing lawyer may find that a commitment to bar association work must always take second place to an urgent motion hour, brief, or trial. A law faculty member that decides to become involved in bar association work may find the opportunity to move up rapidly in the committee structure.

In working with local and state bar associations, keep in mind that there are issues of local politics. It is very easy to become deeply involved in lower level committee work, education programs and publications. Top lawyers in the state, however, will have a structure for electing top members of the association. Breaking into that organization requires working with the politics of that group.

If a faculty member has worked to become an expert in an area through teaching and research, there is another place that service may be rendered. The local news media is always looking for "experts" to comment on breaking news stories. Volunteering to answer questions for the newspaper, radio or television can lead to some exciting opportunities. Once a faculty member has shown a willingness to help, the local media will contact that person every time a story comes up.

Some faculty members fear that the local media will tend to publish harsh comments by and about them. That is rarely true. If the faculty member is being used as an "expert" to comment on topics, the news media is usually very gentle. The reporters will take a quote or two and use them in the story. Since the reporter knows that he or she will need future quotes for future stores, the reporter usually makes every effort to keep the law faculty member happy. Working with the reporters by answering a few questions or even having an interview filmed for the evening news can be fun.

### D. Pro Bono?

Law faculty members have a unique opportunity to make a real difference in the lives of people in the community. With all faculty members having the legal training and many having a law license in the state where they teach, the possibility of doing pro bono work is endless.

The most obvious opportunity for doing pro bono work is volunteering time to well known organizations. Legal Aid, ACLU, Habitat for Humanity and other organizations need volunteer lawyers to provide legal assistance. A law faculty member can select from among many well known organizations and provide service in an area that the faculty member finds interesting.

In addition to those nationally known groups, every community has local organizations that need volunteers. Those organizations may be similar to the national organizations that provide legal services. The local groups may also provide services of a different type. Arts groups, community groups, educational groups, churches and many other activities can use the services of a lawyer as a volunteer or board member. A law faculty member who has spent some time in the community can easily identify a group that is of interest and needs help.

# CHAPTER 8 - VISITING

An earlier chapter noted the possibility of leaving the law school of one's initial appointment and going to a different law school. That is not, of course, necessary and some law faculty members spend their whole careers at one institution. One of the advantages of law school teaching, however, is the opportunity for travel. A law faculty member may decide to remain at one law school, but use it as a base to see the United States and the world. The faculty member may visit at another U.S. law school or look for opportunities to visit at law schools around the world.

## A. Visiting at other U.S. Law School

As noted in an earlier chapter, the possibilities for visiting at another U.S. law school are available. Chapter IV discussed the methods of finding a U.S. law school to visit and should be reviewed if that seems like something a faculty member wants to do. It should be kept in mind that there are actually two types of visits. A faculty member may seek out true visits with the intent of staying for the specified time. In the alternative, a faculty member may go on a "look-see" visit with the thought of possibly staying at the other law school. In fact, a faculty member may go on a true visit with the expectation of returning to his or her home school, only to discover that maybe it is time to look for another place to locate permanently.

Regardless of the type of visit, the faculty member should try to be a good visitor. When on a visit, there may be a tendency to assume that there is no reason to take a great interest in the school being visited. The visiting faculty member may decide to spend most of his or her own time doing some sightseeing, traveling and generally spending time as if on a vacation. The visiting faculty member may assume that showing up for classes is more than enough to satisfy the "visit." That mentality could not be further from the truth.

A faculty member on a visit should make every effort to be seen as a part of the school where the visit is taking place. The same expectations that would apply in the home school should apply in the visited school. The visiting faculty member should be in the law school building for full days. That will allow the students to have the opportunity to ask questions, but it will also allow the faculty of the law school to see the visitor as a colleague.

In addition to being in the building, the visiting faculty member should take extra steps to be a colleague. The easy steps would be to have coffee with the faculty, join the faculty for lunch, and take opportunities to talk with faculty members who teach and research in areas of similar interest. The visitor should also go beyond the easy collegial expectations. The visitor should offer to make a presentation to the faculty, and make a presentation to the alumnae or community. The visitor will also find that a few local faculty members will provide extra service and support during the visit. The visitor should take those people out to dinner and find ways to provide additional thanks.

Being an active colleague will provide benefits in a wide range of ways. Obviously, the visited law school will benefit by having an active colleague in the building. The local faculty members will enjoy the visitor and the students will appreciate a dedicated teacher. The visitor will also benefit. Becoming a part of the local school will allow the visitor to learn more about legal education and the variety of things that can occur. In addition, the visitor will be building a larger set of colleagues and friends for the future. One can never tell when a good reference for future visits or a good co-author for a future research project will be needed. By being a good visitor, the visiting faculty member is adding to the people that can be contacted in the future.

## B. Visiting at International Opportunities

Visiting positions are not limited to the United States. There are many opportunities to visit law schools in other countries. Visits to other countries are a little harder to arrange then U.S. visits but are well worth the effort. The opportunity to travel, learn about foreign law schools, meet foreign law teachers and generally experience foreign culture is exciting.

Many law schools offer summer programs abroad. If a faculty member is lucky enough to be teaching at one of those law schools, then volunteering for that program is the first step to a visit abroad. If that is not possible, the faculty member could begin to contact schools that do offer such programs and try to talk to the person responsible for setting up the program. It may be possible to arrange an invitation to teach in another school's summer program.

There is, of course, the nationally known "Fulbright" program that does offer fellowships for teaching and research abroad. For details about this program, the web site is:

http://www.iie.org

It is then necessary to follow the web site links to Fulbright Programs.

The Fulbright program is not limited to law school faculty members. It is, instead, a broad program for all areas of teaching and research with some limited opportunities for law scholars. It requires a close reading of all of the materials in order to determine the programs that are appropriate for any individual candidate. The application and acceptance program is detailed and close scrutiny of the program requirements is necessary in order to obtain such a fellowship.

In short, a faculty member has many opportunities to become a visiting professor at another school. Consider those options if you want a permanent change or a temporary, short term appointment.

# CHAPTER 9 - LOOKING AT RETIREMENT

The first part of the book talked about getting that first law teaching job. This last chapter is intended to bring the story full circle. If a person has spent his or her whole career in law school teaching, then there will come a time when thinking about retirement is a good idea. As with most careers, thinking about leaving work is something most people put off as long as possible. Law teaching is such a rewarding career many law teachers stay as long as possible. There are some things about retirement, however, that should be considered.

### A. You Never have to Stop Working

The first thing that can be noted about retirement from law teaching is that it is not really necessary. A law professor never has to stop working. The skills, talents and projects that are started during a law teaching career can last a lifetime. In addition, the actual job may be held for a long time.

With modern age discrimination statutes, it is not possible for law schools to set arbitrary retirement ages. A law teacher, therefore, does not have to automatically retire at 65 or 70. It should also be noted that law school teaching and research is not physically demanding. For a person in relatively good health, the physical demands of teaching and research can be met in the years well past 70. It should be noted, however, there may be some resistance from others to that practice.

A more senior faculty member will find that others on the faculty may start looking to ease out the senior faculty as they get older. It is sometimes viewed that more senior faculty are resistant to change, will not adopt new ideas, and take up large salaries while doing less work. Some junior faculty and deans may hope to free up large salary lines in order to hire younger faculty members. Such ideas will probably not be openly expressed, are usually incorrect and boarding on age discrimination. A senior faculty member should, however, be aware of what the colleagues are thinking.

There are a few ways to avoid having colleagues constantly suggesting that it is time to go. The most obvious method of avoiding that problem is to continue working. When younger colleagues see a senior faculty member teaching large classes, serving on major committees and then continuing to publish more then the junior members of the faculty, it removes the reasons for the talk. In addition, it allows the senior faculty member to be a good roll model for the rest of the faculty.

If a faculty member decides to retire from full time teaching that does not mean that the faculty member has to stop working completely. There are many parts of the law teaching career that can be continued for many years after leaving a full time position.

For the faculty member that has decided to stop full time teaching, the possibility of serving as an adjunct remains. Many older faculty members retire and then return to the same law school to teach one or two classes a semester. That retired faculty member does not have to serve on committees and does not have to continue to publish. It allows the faculty member to remain active and provide a needed class to the school.

For the faculty member that was an active scholar during the teaching career, research and publications can continue. A faculty member may continue to update books that were published or continue writing law review articles in the area of interest.

Some faculty members decide to move after retirement. It should be remembered that there are law schools all over the country. Many of them are located in geographical areas where the climate is moderate year round. A retired faculty member may seek to form some relationship with a law school in a new area. Such a relationship will allow the retired faculty member to use the library, remain up to date on issues of interest, and form bonds with colleagues at the new law school.

### B. Preparing for Retirement

For the faculty member that does decide to retire, there are additional issues to address. General preparation for retirement is well beyond the scope of this book. There are many sources available that give advice and a faculty member should begin seeking information early. It is unfortunate to see a senior faculty member wanting to retire but uncertain how to accomplish that feat because of a lack of planning. Most universities and investment organizations provide retirement counseling. The law faculty member should seek that advice early.

In addition to gaining financial advice, there are some additional things a law faculty member should consider in planning for retirement. For a person who has spent his or her career teaching and researching, coming to a complete stop can be troubling. Most law teachers want to have some way to continue to think and work within the areas that have been important throughout the career. The previous section suggested several alternatives for the retired faculty member that wants to stay busy. Those are, of course, not the only ones available. The key to being happy in retirement is planning for it. Just as a law faculty member will have to plan for the financial aspects of retirement, that person will have to plan for the emotional and mental aspects of retirement. The faculty member should begin early thinking about what keeps his or her mind occupied. It may be research, some teaching, old hobbies or new hobbies. A retired faculty member may decide, for example, that he or she will want to spend retirement writing supplements to books in the morning and walking on the beach in the afternoons. Carefully planning years before retirement can make that happen.

Observing faculty members as they get older, reveals one interesting point. Most law faculty members have the financial ability to retire at a fairly young age. Most, however, do not know what they will do after they leave full time teaching. Many would like to leave the full time job, but have a fear of having nothing to do. That fear keeps many on the job longer then they would really like to be. That aspect or retirement should be a part of the planning at a point even earlier then the financial part.

CPSIA information can be obtained at www.ICGtesting.com
Printed in the USA
LVOW051204150212

268785LV00002B/7/P

9 781600 420511